FLOWERS and SYMBOLS
for the CHRISTIAN YEAR

FLOWERS
and SYMBOLS
for the
CHRISTIAN YEAR

by Ruth E. Mullins

HEARTHSIDE PRESS, INC., PUBLISHERS
NEW YORK

Dedicated to

my garden club friends and church women who use their
time and talent to beautify their churches and their homes

and to my devoted husband, Major A. R. Mullins, who took good
care of me while this book was in preparation.

Acknowledgments

I would like to express my appreciation to:

Mr. and Mrs. Edwin Adkins; Rev. and Mrs. Z. C. Adkins; the Altar Guild and the Flower Committee of Trinity Methodist Church, DeLand, Florida; Mrs. Edna Barrett; Mrs. Ethelyn Baird, Librarian, City Library of DeLand, Florida; Mrs. Bernice Clements; Mrs. Mary Gardner; Mrs. Ellen Griffen; Mrs. Graham King; Mr. and Mrs. John Lang; Mrs. Amy Lau; Mrs. Arla MacDonald; Mrs. Betty Nielson; Mr. and Mrs. Allen Powers; Mrs. Walter Ruhlman; Mrs. Mattie Mae Shields; Miss Charlotte Smith, Librarian, Stetson University; Mrs. Elaine Waidelich; Mrs. Evelyn West; Mr. H. V. Westervelt; Mrs. Taylor Workman; Mrs. Maggie Wright; Mrs. Guy Yaste;

The photographers: Mrs. Lenance Robinette Clark, Mr. Horace Heley, Mr. George Kniska of the Madell Studio, Mr. Howard T. Powell; also, for other photographs, *Akron Beacon-Journal;* Dan Brazell Studio; C. Fanders; Jackson & Perkins Co.; Kent Studio; Photo-Art Studio, Inc.; Press Bureau of Delray Beach; Walden Photos, Inc. Plates 1 and 3 courtesy of the American Craftsmen's Council and the craftsmen; plates 5, 13-16, 18, and 20 courtesy of R. A. Newhouse, Inc.

My church and garden club friends, who have been a source of inspiration, encouragement and helpfulness and to all who urged me to put in written form these lectures and arrangements which have been used in garden clubs and churches;

Dr. Paul K. Wheeler, Professor of English, Stetson University;

Julie Noonan for all drawings, except where otherwise noted;

and Nedda Anders, my editor, and Hearthside Press, my publisher, for immeasurable help, encouragement, and inspiration from the time this book was first conceived until its ultimate publication.

Contents

FLOWERS and SYMBOLS
for the CHRISTIAN YEAR

I

New Trends, New Needs

Sing unto the Lord a new song, and his praise from the end of the earth. Isaiah 42:10

The widespread need for a simple book on flower arrangements with a religious theme, written with special regard for new trends in architecture, art, liturgy, and symbolism, has occasioned this book. It is presented with the hope that it will be useful to altar guilds, church youth leaders, garden club and women's groups, and all who wish to create more meaningful arrangements to mark the days and occasions of the Christian year—at home or in public places.

The new spirit in the church stresses fuller involvement of the church member in the service. Young people particularly, their tastes conditioned by op art, pop art, junk assemblages, and happenings, must be reached in a language they understand. In creating modern arrangements in their design idiom, we confirm that the church is theirs as well as ours. Symbolism, too, can help these youngsters find relevance in the church, for were not early Christians who used the everyday fish form of pagan life as a secret symbol for Jesus Christ thereby celebrating the ordinary and the commonplace, exactly as the junk assemblager does today?

But flowers are for people of all ages; their value in bringing an emotional aspect to the religious experience is well understood. Living flowers and plants bring to the service a heightened awareness of the mood and meaning of the occasion. And this response is sharpened when the varied and beautiful symbolic content of the arrangement is understood. The design elements of color, line, and shape, as explained in the following chapter, can be used to create a mood appropriate to the event. Representational figurines can be included as accessories. Plants which have religious significance because of their association with the Bible can be the grace notes of the composition. But whatever the decoration, information about its symbolism should be made available to the viewers by members of the Altar Guild.

This book is about the search for creative meaning through arrangement. Arranging for the Christian year should and can be as varied and beautiful as the art and history of the church itself. It seems to me, however, that there has been a noticeable failure among many altar guilds and church service groups to make the most of the opportunities open to them in using flowers. Flowers are so pleasing in themselves that their mere presence is apt to seem satisfactory to those who have not become aware of their potential as a medium for creativity. Many altar guilds tend to have a standing order with a florist, sending over to him glass fillers for the brass containers to be filled with "large flowers" for the sanctuary, "small ones" for the nave. This order may be further pinned down to "white flowers" for Confirmation Sundays, lilies for Easter, poinsettias for Christmas, and perhaps "blue flowers" for Pentecost. In other words, the ladies of the committee have a general idea of the way they want the church to look on certain days, but they often leave most of the joy of creation to the florist and concentrate on keeping the vases shining and the altar cloths trim.

Occasionally a talented member of the congregation will make a special arrangement using flowers from her garden, or an arrangement that has won a prize at a flower show will be repeated for the church or home, but it is paradoxical that so few women grow flowers for the church, since interest in gardening increases all the time. Although there are few members these days with great estates and crews of gardeners to fill the church with flowers, there are many more with carefully tended small gardens, many more members of the congregation who are also members of garden clubs. Growing flowers for the church—God's garden—perhaps including some plants of special symbolism, can be a richly spiritual experience and an opportunity also to educate the youngsters in the community.

Another reason why we must reshape our ideas about flower arranging and worship is that the physical world around us is changing. Indeed, it is a source of constant amazement to those who equate the church with conservatism that the churches are among the structures that most break with tradition. Not that our traditional churches do not occupy a large part of our hearts! The magnificent Gothic spires and multi-colored windows of old cathedrals in the cities, the soaring points of white wood towers against the rural landscape, even the old-fashioned "American Gothic" village church covered with Victorian gingerbread all are central to our lives and deserve the best in the flower arranger's art.

But we must note that in the years since World War II a trend towards modernism in houses of worship has developed.

CONTEMPORARY ARCHITECTURE

Perhaps the most recurring purpose of the modern church architect is to get away from the massive materials and heavy mood of the Gothic styles. New churches and new houses aim at lightness. Getting away from the comparatively static shape of the box, topped by the familiar spire or set off by columns, they attempt a more dynamic structure, one that connotes a feeling of expansion of time and space. The range of styles is wide. There are the buildings of glass with a visible skeletal construction . . . the churches and houses that are "sculptures"—flowing structures of pre-cast concrete . . . or the windowless, fortress-like buildings such as the First Unitarian Church of Rochester, New York, designed by Paul Rudolph and Louis Kahn.

There are modern churches that are planned to take advantage of a site, such as St. Philip's in the Hills in Tucson, Arizona, where a giant picture window provides a rear altar view of the Catalina Mountains.

New design provides us with such truly novel churches as that in Stockton, California, for example, where the Central Methodist Church deliberately sought "an inspirational form that would not be too formal or cathedral-like." Architects Anschen and Allen found their solution in great pre-cast concrete bents supporting a structure that rises from twenty-five feet at the lowest point of its tent-like roof to eighty-five feet above the altar. The roof is heavy wood planking exposed on the inside and covered with thick redwood shakes outside.

Eero Saarinen's design for the North Christian Church in Columbus, Indiana, used a hexagon, and the result was a striking interior. Since the Disciples of Christ service is centered on communion, of which everyone partakes, the pews are arranged around the Lord's Table in the middle of the sanctuary, lighted by a skylight above. Liturgical colors—purple, white, green and red—predominate, and the organ pipes are used as a backdrop for the altar. Two large candelabra with topiary greenery flank the altar. The First Methodist Church in Orlando, Florida, places the pulpit in the center surrounded by the altar.

Hartford, Connecticut; Seattle, Washington; New Orleans, Louisiana; Palos Verdes, California; Alexandria, Virginia—all have unusually striking new "visible expressions of man's faith," to quote *Fortune* magazine which in December, 1964, spoke of the "constant re-examination and re-statement of church builders" as they "strive to interpret, in contemporary terms, man's view of his relationship with God." "Church design," says *Fortune,* "must now foster the sense, as well as the fact of participation. With the churchly re-emphasis on essentials, architects find a new freedom to use basic materials—wood, brick, concrete, steel—in their unadorned forms."

NEW STYLES IN CHURCH INTERIORS

Such church buildings call for new approaches to ornamentation, too, and today's church shows stained glass windows in abstract designs executed by craftsmen using techniques hundreds of years old. Altar hangings display contemporary needlecraft and stylized designs of liturgical symbols and flowers. Pulpits, baptismal fonts, pews, even the communion rail, are designed by contemporary craftsmen with today's fabrics and materials, and woven screens of metal, wood or fabric give a new feeling to the sanctuary. Plate 1 shows the handsome modern interior of the Church of the Redeemer in Baltimore, Maryland. A magnificent hanging altar cross designed and executed by Ronald Hayes Pearson is a focus in a setting which creates a mood of awe and reverence.

The chapel at the Massachusetts Institute of Technology in Cambridge, another Saarinen design, is a windowless cylinder which stands in a water-filled moat. Its altar is a solid marble rectangular pedestal about three feet high. Behind it, illuminated from above, is a screen by sculptor Harry Bertoia, not a solid partition, but an open fret of slim metal rods and cross plates.

Plate 1

This chapel, which is used interdenominationally, is essentially simple. The chairs, which are not fixed to the floor, have the spare look of Quaker furniture. The richness of the interior comes from natural details such as sunlight from the window above the moat reflecting from the water and appearing to dance on the stone walls. In this atmosphere, any flower arrangement stands out powerfully. It must be perfect in balance and form; it may be a heavy mass design or it may be linear and intricate in detail, but it should have a symbolic life of its own.

A CHANGING VIEW OF FLOWER ARRANGEMENT

Just as contemporary designers and sculptors have found it necessary to invent new shapes and patterns for church fittings and furniture, new patterns for applied decorations, and new materials for interiors, our churches and our homes require a new way of thinking about arrangements.

For example, new furniture is more apt to be designed "in the round" than was traditional furniture. This is because our rooms are constructed more openly, with more glass areas, and people no longer tend to square their furniture off with the walls. Many new churches are designed in this way. The sanctuary, the communion table, are centered in the main body of the church, and the pews surround them on all four sides. Thus an altar table arrangement, for example, might have to be designed in the round, since it would be freestanding. Flowers for home arrangements must also relate to new architecture. A table in a foyer with a circular hanging staircase must be attractive from four sides as well as from above; a design which stands on a room divider separating living and dining areas must look handsome from both areas. Line and form become more important than ever. Framed against the vast expanses of glass in some churches, where the world outside becomes a part of the world within, insignificant arrangements will only be distracting, and great showy arrangements are needed. New thinking is sometimes required. For the interior of a modern church in Connecticut, whose pulpit stands are silhouetted in winter and summer against a backdrop of tall trees, lavish baskets overflowing with flowers and vines are suspended from the exposed wood ceiling beams.

Plate 2 shows the modern interior of the First Methodist Church, Orlando, Florida, with the altar at left, the pulpit at right. On the woven linen altar cloth are twelve tongues of fire, symbolizing the Pentecost; symbolism is also seen in the stained glass windows. Flowers raised on a standard in a simple mass design are effective against this detailed background. Generally, masses of flowers should be used against highly textured or ornamented walls, including brick and hewn wood.

Contrast in texture, mood, and color is vital to modern design, and echoing the materials used or blending subtly with the colors may be exactly the wrong thing to do. Thin line arrangements may be lost, as may be arrangements using heavy containers and foliage in the manner of the building. In many of the arrangements shown here, it is the very old-fashionedness of traditional flowers, the delicacy and softness, that gives the needed contrast in texture and mood. Even the simplicity of contemporary design brings out, by contrast, the loveliness of the complexity of natural forms in flower and foliage.

Plate 2

What is changing so much about flower arrangement for religious purposes is that we have a new freedom to choose whatever path we desire. If we feel that using a modern interpretative arrangement of materials that are new to church arrangement—wild flowers and foliage, dried materials—will best express a religious theme, we may do so without fear of offense, even in the most elaborately ornamented traditional churches.

And, on the other hand, if we wish to employ the always beautiful triangles and crescent forms of traditional ecclesiastical arrangement, we may do that too. Whatever best helps us to communicate, "to sing for the honor of His name . . . to make His praise glorious," (Psalms 66:2) is fitting. We may, and should, use a greater variety of accessories, of containers, of backgrounds to tell our story, and we may do so knowing that we are entirely reverent and are using our creativity to bring to arrangement a personal involvement with our churches.

This new spirit in flower arrangement is just beginning. One can imagine so many forms it may take, so many directions to follow. In secular arrangements we are beginning to experiment with such diverse ideas as pop art, assemblage, abstract sculpture, welded art. Bas-relief painting, op art, mobiles, stabiles, constructivism—all these fads and manners of modern art have become familiar to flower arrangers. We must now bring this creativity to our church arrangements.

NATURAL FORMS IN ARRANGEMENT

We are now arranging the forms of nature that we pick up on our walks and trips through the countryside—the driftwood and interesting stones and fungi and leaves. But as the church becomes more deeply associated with the urban modern world, the junk of our city scrapyards and the steel and chrome of its vehicles and buildings will become employed increasingly in flower arrangement just as it has already in mid-century American art.

ART IN ARRANGEMENT

We can do so much more with our arrangements by going back to the paintings, the etchings, the magnificent triptychs and murals, the sculpture of the past. We are all much too prone to use the statuary that has been made available commercially. The over-familiar figurines of monks, cupids, and Madonnas that we call upon so repeatedly should be replaced by more inspired designs. In place of what has become trite and sentimental, we must learn to draw upon the vast treasure house of the church . . . the polychromed wood Christs of the Twelfth Century, the sculpture on the Romanesque pedestals of the medieval churches, the French Renaissance bright gilded altar pieces and the famous tapestries. All of this great art of the past can furnish inspiration for new designs of significant worth, so too can the folk art of the past and present. Woven crosses from South America, Mexican tin ware and pottery figurines all have great character and color and can satisfy our need for more beautiful objects to use in religious worship.

Similarly, we must follow the trend that already exists in secular arrangement, and make our containers more meaningful, more a whole with the plant material and a valuable aspect of the design. Brass, silver, and gold containers to match the altar fittings are always beautiful, and many are designed by contemporary craftsmen. But reproductions of historic chalices and goblets, creative designs made with craft materials reproducing symbols of the church, and the use of objects which themselves have liturgical symbolism will enhance our arrangements.

We must urge commercial studios to give us more fine reproductions of such art and of contemporary religious paintings and sculpture. If manufacturers of jig-saw puzzles can reproduce great paintings of old and new masters, surely there is no reason why good reproductions should not be made available for altar-guild use.

Finally, the new freedom calls for a greater use of flowers, foliage, and plants throughout the church. Our classrooms are often as important as our chapels, and particularly where children are involved one should call forth the magic of flowers to communicate. The minister's study, where he helps so many people both from within his congregation and from outside it; the meeting rooms, where the good works of the church go on; the narthex or vestry, where the visitor to the church gains his first impression; the chancels and chapels, where the important ceremonies of life are carried on—all these places receive attention from the members of the church whose service it is to furnish arrangments. No matter what its period or style of design, there is no church, no corner of the church, that cannot benefit from finer flower arrangements.

NEW AND OLD TRENDS IN THE CHURCH YEAR

Although the eight seasons of the Christian year, their colors, and the symbolism associated with them will be discussed in detail throughout this volume, the following introductory material is pertinent.

The Christian liturgical season was based on the ritual of worship established by the religions which preceded them. Since the earliest Christians were converted Jews, it was natural for them to work out a plan of worship inspired by the Judaic rituals. Thus, they compiled a calendar of festal days and seasons, which were gradually elaborated into a pageant of Christian tradition.

The Episcopal, Lutheran, and Catholic Churches have followed traditional patterns of observance, and most of the references to liturgical churches in this book would have application to their present-day practices.

But during the Reformation, many of the saint's days and other feasts antithetical to the Protestant conscience were given up, and with the rise of Puritanism even Christmas and Easter were abandoned for a while. Today, however, the tendency is to restate basic beliefs through the use of liturgy. On a local level, at the discretion of individual clergymen, some of the rich practices of ancient Protestantism are being restored, and there is a strong movement in modern seminaries towards a more ritualistic religion.

One of the points of genius of the church year, says Robert Wetzler in *Seasons and Symbols, A Handbook on the Church Year,* is that "It is an ongoing pageant, bringing to mind those historic events of two thousand years ago, connecting them with a history of the Jews which preceded, and a history of Christianity which resulted. The church year, in short, associates us with God's activities and with that mighty cloud of witnesses which has gone before us, inspiring us to be Christ's mighty arm against the foe in our time. The church year is a pageant, yet more than a pageant. It is life itself—life in Christ unfolded before us in a comprehensible sequence packed with meaning."

II

Christian Symbolism

Symbol—that which stands for or suggests something else by reason of relationship, association, convention or accidental . . . resemblance . . . esp. a visible sign of something invisible, as an idea, a quality, or totality such as a state or a church; an emblem . . . Merriam-Webster Unabridged Dictionary, Second Edition

In the last few decades, many architects, artists, and craftsmen who design objects for ecclesiastial use have drawn on the rich heritage of Christian symbolism for their inspiration, overlooking no part of the church in their desire to create structures which are meaningful and appropriate for reverent worship. Plate 3 shows church doors adorned with eloquent circular "sermons in bronze." The circle itself, being never-ending, is a symbol that God is eternal.

Mrs. J. Burton Nichols of Wilmington, Delaware, who designed and executed the door medallions, explains their symbolism:

The twenty bronze medallions on the front doors are symbolic of the four Gospels. Their arrangement in columns and rows is significant of their interrelated message. The top row introduces the four evangelists: Mark, Matthew, Luke and John. The column under each depicts teachings symbolic of each Gospel writer. The second row represents each evangelist's unique introduction to his Gospel. The distinctive relationship of Christ to the message of the Old Testament revelation and tradition is told in the third row. The fourth row of symbols described the relationship between Christ and the believer, which is established through the New Covenant. The bottom row gives each evangelist's interpretation of Christ's redemptive passion.

The half border on each panel, which guides the viewer's eye along each column, is significant of the character of each Gospel narrative.

The Gospel of Mark, because it was written first, is placed in the left column. The *winged lion* represents the "voice of one crying in the wilderness." With power and vigor Mark's gospel witnesses to the Christ Whom God reveals. The strength of Christ's will as it was forged to the will of God is represented in the *chain border*. *The Dove* is the symbol of the Holy Spirit which descended upon Jesus at His baptism. *The Flame, Burning Bush,* and *Flaming Wheel* point to the Transfiguration of Christ, where His relationship to the Law and the Prophets was established. The Law, given through Moses, is shown in the burning bush. The Prophets are represented through Elijah whose symbol is the fiery wheel. God's voice is shown in the single flame. *The Palm, Corner Stone* and *Sword* tell of Christ's reception and welcome into the Holy City. His later rejection, and of God's judgment upon those who chose to reject Him. *The Cross* and *Nimbus,* significant of Christ's passion and death, give witness to the world in the words of the Centurion, "Truly, this man was the Son of God."

The symbols of St. Matthew are placed in the second column. *The Winged Man* is symbolic of Matthew's gospel because of the emphasis on the lineal descent of Jesus from Abraham. *The Rope* border represents Matthew's close tie of the Old and New Testaments. *The Seven-Branch Candlestick,* traditional symbol of Judaism, shows Jesus in His relationship to God and His chosen people. *The Alpha and Omega, Tablets of Stone* and *The Scroll* proclaim that Jesus is the Beginning and the Ending, that He came to fulfill the Law and the Prophets. *The Boat and The Fish* convey Matthew's concept of the way faith becomes a reality. The boat represents the Church and the fish the believers in Christ. *The Crown and Sign,* Matthew's symbol of Christ's passion, show the first letters of the Latin words of Pilate's inscription on the Cross, INRI, which mean, "Jesus of Nazareth, the King of the Jews."

St. Luke's gospel is represented by the *Winged Ox,* telling of the sacrifice of Jesus for our redemption and also of the gentle strength of the evangelist himself. *The Thorn* edging of the medallions shows Luke's emphasis upon the suffering of Christ. *The Horn of Oil and Pomegranate* symbolize healing and salvation and the propagation of the Gospel, the resurrection and the hope of immortality. *The Cross of Healing and the Star of David* tell of Luke's conception of Christ's mission of redemption to God's people. *The Fountain, Branches and Birds* show Luke's presentation of the New Convenant. The Fountain of Life is Christ, the Birds, believers from both Jewish and Gentile peoples, and the Branches, one broken, the other whole, tell of Christ's salvation to all who believe in Him. *The Crown of Thorns and The Nails* depict the vicarious suffering of Christ's redemptive act for our salvation.

The Winged Eagle, traditional symbol of St. John and his gospel, characterizes the lofty, soaring, and powerful message of one whose true home is in the heights of heaven. *The Vine* symbolizes Life in Christ, a thought which permeates the whole gospel of John. *The Agnus Dei,* the Lamb of God, tells of the Triumph of Christ which John announces at the very beginning of his narrative. *The Grapes and Wheat,* significant of the elements of the Sacrament of the Altar, show the sacramental character of the whole gospel. *The Vine and Branches* are symbols of the new relationship through faith in Christ. It contains the shields of the twelve apostles, who, with all who believe, find the living source of their life in Christ, the Vine. *The Passion Flower*, the corona of which represents the Crown of Thorns, together with the stamens and pistils representing the nails of the Cross, and the five sepals and five petals, pointing to the ten faithful apostles, all, in a beautiful manner, as a flower in full bloom, portray the suffering of Christ, discipleship and beauty of life.

Plate 3

The study of symbology is engrossing in itself, but it must be made clear that except for certain familiar symbols (representations of religious figures or such widely understood signs as the dove, lamb, etc.) it is difficult, even impossible, to communicate through them unless the spectator is made aware of their meaning. To this end, flower-show schedule writers, altar guild volunteers, garden-club members, and all who seek to use symbolism should disseminate information through every means available. Releases to newspapers and radio media, notices in internal publications, printed cards accompanying flower-show exhibits, informal talks at home and in the class rooms—all of these methods should be used. As an understanding of Christian symbolism develops, the Bible will more than ever become a source of strength and inspiration. And the opportunity to be creative through a knowledge of Christian symbolism with its complex link to Judaism and other religions will become greater and more challenging than ever.

The roots of Christian symbolism lie in many cultures. Egyptian religion and hieroglyphics gave shape to man's awareness that his world was both spiritual and material, natural and cultural. The Chaldeans, the Syrians, and the Phoenicians added to the art and myths of the Greeks which set the stage for Christian moral principles, concepts of natural laws, and the great contrasts which determine cosmic and human life as, for example, the yearly decay and revival of life. In addition, there was a stream of oriental influence from the East and from the practices and beliefs of Hebraic culture.

Early Christians used secret symbols to communicate with other Christians. The Catacombs of Rome are filled with carvings of fish, the secret sign for Jesus Christ, and the fish symbol was repeated in carvings and on medals carried by Christians as a means of identification.

In his writings, St. Augustine expressed the belief that symbols fed and stirred the fires of logic, enabling Man to excel himself. He also discussed the value of all things in nature as bearers of spiritual messages by virtue of their distinctive forms and characteristics.

J. E. Circlot, in *A Dictionary of Symbolism,* says "Most of the classical Fathers of the church have something to say about symbolism and since they enjoyed such a high reputation in Roman times, one can see why this was the period when the symbol came to be so deeply experienced, loved and understood."

The Old and New Testaments contain many references to symbols both in prophecy and fulfillment. Jesus said "I am the vine and ye are the branches;" we interpret "vine" to mean Christ, and "branches" to mean His followers. Thus, we use actual materials such as vines and bare branches as a pictorial representation, the visible form of an abstract statement.

Medieval churches used symbols as visual aids in education, giving every symbol a meaning beyond its decorative purpose. Printing had to be done by hand and was very expensive, and many of the congregation were unlettered; therefore, religion was taught with paintings, drawings, and by other graphic means. During the Crusades, banners and armor emblazoned with symbols were used to carry the message of the church. And during the Renaissance, symbolism was much employed by the poets and painters. Stained glass windows of our churches were enshrined with symbols which taught the immortal and imperishable truths of the Gospel of Christ and His Church, and carvings too recorded and described His passion, death and resurrection.

In our own time there has been a huge upsurge of interest in symbology. Social scientists, anthropologists, and psychologists have sought in symbology the interpretations of man's dreams. Painters such as Salvador Dali have used Christian symbols to express a world of fantasy; architects of new churches use symbolism to achieve a closer link between worshipper and his religion. In fact, all modern art speaks in the language of signs. At a modern ballet or drama, for example, no real story is told; instead, the characters move representationally, suggesting some inner feeling rather than acting out a sequence of related events.

THE LANGUAGE OF FLOWERS AND PLANTS OF THE BIBLE

Horticulturists and Bible authorities have tried for many centuries to identify the actual plants mentioned in the Bible, but the scientific system of naming plants is no more than 250 years old. Therefore, one cannot always be sure that the plants as we know them today are the ones which the Bible mentioned. For example, the Biblical rose of Sharon is the flower we recognize as the tulip, the sword lily is our gladiolus. Some Biblical names are general. Corn, for instance, alludes to various grains, not to maize or Indian corn, which was unknown in Bible times. This difficulty with plant identification is further compounded by the fact that translating the Bible from ancient Hebrew and Greek texts has resulted in many different versions, and the difference of opinion extends to plants as well as to other matters.

Although the following sections list primarily the plants of the Bible, I have included a few, like the rose, which have developed a special symbolism through long usage. Again, I urge flower arrangers and altar guild members who are using these materials symbolically to explain their meanings, for sign language can be a means of communication only when it is understood by the hearers as well as the speakers.

Even within the limiting framework imposed by the subject there is still plenty of room for the exercise of imagination when selecting flowers for religious occasions. The common names of flowers often suggest ways in which to use them. For example, bridal wreath (*Spiraea prunifolia* or *S. vanhouttei*) for weddings, babies'-breath for Madonna and Child designs, and many many others. Obvious resemblances can be drawn on, as in using *Mentzelia decapetel,* commonly called evening star flower, in association with references to stars.

Acacia—The Ark of the Covenant was made from the wood of a species of acacia and all Biblical references to shittim wood mean the wood of this *shittah* tree. Some students believe that this tree could have been the burning bush under which Moses was resting when God called to him.

Almond—In Jerusalem the almond tree bursts into sudden bloom early in the year, and for this reason it came to symbolize awakening and revival. Jeremiah 1:11 used it in this sense. A widely used motif in sacred carvings. Exodus 25:33.

Aloe (Aloe succotrina)—Used for embalming and purifying the dead. John 19:39 relates that Nicodemus brought a mixture of myrrh and aloe, to the burial of Jesus.

Anemone—Bible references to lilies of the field have been interpreted as meaning many different flowers, since the true white lily is rare in Palestine. Violets, lily of the valley, waterlilies and amaryllis are among those which have been suggested. But most modern authorities believe that the anemone, found throughout Palestine, best fits the various Biblical mentions of lilies of the field.

Anthurium—Symbolizes the heart (from Luther's coat of arms).

Apples—Apple trees being practically unknown in Palestine, the references to apples are usually said to mean apricots or figs.

Aspalathus—Fragrant shrub of the pea family to which the wisdom of the Lord was likened.

Barley—Variously used as a symbol either of poverty (2. Kings 7:16) or of jealousy (Numbers 5:15), because barley flour is inferior to flour made from wheat. The miracle of the loaves (John 6:9) featured barley. So perhaps the symbolism here could be "blessed are the lowly"?

Bay Leaves (Laurus nobilis)—These come from the true laurel of history. They were used in ancient medicine; from such use might have developed its association with mourning, and reference to the burial of Jesus with spices.

Bean—In ancient days, a white bean signified a yes vote; a black bean a no vote.

Bitter Herbs—Passover symbol in the Jewish faith, eaten as a reminder of the bitterness of bondage. Dandelion, chicory, lettuce, cress, sorrel, mint, eryngium, etc., were appropriate. However, bitter herbs are not mentioned in Gospel story of The Last Supper.

Boxwood (Buxus)—"I will set in the desert the fir tree, and the pine, and the box tree together: that they may see . . . that the hand of the Lord hath done this . . ." Isaiah 41:19. Represents abiding grace and prosperity of the Church of God.

Bramble—Usually interpreted to mean any thorny plant, but some authorities say that the original reference is to *Rubus ulmifolius*.

Bulrush (Cyperus papyrus)—was used in Egypt for making paper, hence its name. This is supposed to be the plant from which Moses' Ark was made (Ex. 2:3).

Burning Bush (Loranthus acacae)—(Crimson-flowered mistletoe) Ex. 3:2. God called to Moses out of the burning bush. Symbol of giving of the Law.

Carnation—In cultivation two thousand years, early German poets use it as a symbol of the Virgin. It suggests first love and is now used as the symbol of Mother's Day.

Carob—The leathery pods were food for animals.

Castor Bean or Castor-oil Plant (Ricinus communis)—A striking plant with poisonous seeds, it has leaves divided by several lobes; called *Palma christi* in Spanish countries. See Gourd.

Cedar—"The righteous . . . shall grow like a cedar in Lebanon" . . . Pslams 91:12. *Cedrus libani* is frequently mentioned in the Bible, but some biblical references to cedar may mean a closely related and similar tree, *C. deodara,* which has a very durable wood. Symbolizes vigorous steadfastness, and uncorruptible faith, but occasionally represents God's ability to weaken the strong.

Cherry Blossom—Almost all modern varieties derived from two Old World species of *Prunus.* Symbolizes friendliness.

Chestnut—If you are planning an interpretation of Genesis 30:37 or Ezekiel 31:8, and are a purist to the extent of using the actual material intended by the biblical reference, it may interest you to know that the chestnut tree is not grown in Palestine. Some scholars interpret the material as the plane tree.

Chinese Evergreen (Aglaonema simplex)—Symbolizes long life.

Christmas Rose (Helleborus Niger)—Because it blooms at Christmas time, early Christians adopted it as a holy symbol. Represents the Nativity. It grew on Mt. Helicon, the mythical home of Apollo and the Muses.

Chrysanthemum—Cultivated for two thousand years, it shares honors with the cherry blossom as the national flower of Japan, where it symbolizes fruitfulness. Also stands for long life.

Clover—Druids held it sacred; Greeks used it in garlands. Three-leaved clover is emblematic of the Trinity; four-leaved ones are symbols of good fortune.

Coconut—Fruit of the coco palm, probably the most valuable tree in existence, since every part of it can be used in some way, the coconut has been respected since before Christ. It symbolizes endless summer.

Columbine—In Italian art, it is the flower of the dove (Columba is Latin for dove); also the sacred symbol of the Holy Ghost.

Corn—No doubt a general term for cereals of all kinds according to many Bible authorities. Represents the seven gifts of the spirit. In Renaissance legend, these were Faith, Hope, Charity, Justice, Prudence, Temperance, and Strength.

Crape Myrtle (Lagerstroemia Indica)—Longlasting.

clover

Crocus—Sweet, fragrant plant praised in Song of Songs.

Cucumber—Israelites led from Egypt spoke longingly of this plant as a treat.

Cypress—Since early times the cypress tree (*Cupressus sempervirens*) of classical literature has been a symbol of mourning. More recently, symbolic of immortality. Sometimes a symbol of the righteous man who preserves his faith.

Daisy (Bellis perennis)—The English daisy of literature symbolizes innocence.

Dandelion—Cultivated for medicine, it symbolizes the Passion. One of the bitter herbs of Passover.

Date palm tree—Resurrection.

Dianthus—Symbol of divine love.

Dill (Anethum graveolens)—An ancient and valued flavorant and medicinal, scripture refers to this plant as anise. Dill grows easily from seed in most parts of the United States. See Plate 4.

Dogwood (Cornus Florida)—Legend has it that this was the tree on which Christ was crucified. It pitied his suffering, whereupon Christ promised that never again would any dogwood grow large enough to be used for such a purpose. Dogwood blossoms form a cross, thus symbolize the cross of crucifixion. Check state conservation lists before using branches in exhibition—dogwood trees are on the conservation lists in some states.

Plate 4

Easter Lily (Lilium longiflorum)—Life and resurrection.

Elm—The tree of Hosea 4:13 cannot be identified. Perhaps the poplar or pine?

Evergreens—Signify life everlasting because they retain their colors and leaves.

Fig—One of the first fruits of the Bible, sometimes seen as symbol of lust, from Adam's fall from grace, sometimes as symbol of peace and prosperity (I Kings 4:25).

Fir—Choice. A green sanctioned by long usage for Advent, Christmas, etc. Horticulturists translate references to fir as general term for conifers such as cypress and pine.

Frankincense—A gift of the Magi, it represents Divine love.

Fruit—Fruit is the first food mentioned in the Bible, (Ex. 23:39). "Thou shalt not delay to offer the first of thy ripe fruits." Also Jesus refers to the fruit of the Spirit.

Gardenia—This Old World plant is said to represent chastity and femininity.

Gladiolus—(Sushan in Hebrew) Abundance, generosity. Also, the Incarnation, the taking on of human form by Jesus, Son of God.

Glastonbury Thorn—It is said that St. Joseph of Arimathea, who found the first church in England, rested his staff in Somerset; it rooted and became the Glastonbury thorn (a species of hawthorn) which blooms on Christmas Eve, hence represents the Nativity.

Gourd—Signified death and resurrection. Some translators believe that the plant which sprang up over Jonah was a gourd; others say it was the castor bean plant mentioned earlier.

Grape—Frequently named in the Bible, "the vine;" symbolizes the blood of Christ in Holy Communion. Also twelve bunches of grapes on the great Chalice of Antioch represent the twelve apostles. In art and literature, grape stands for revelry and joy.

Grass—A general term for many different varieties. Grass has a relatively short life in Palestine, and most authorities believe that references can best be interpreted to mean fortune is fleeting "like grass which groweth up; in the morning it flourisheth and groweth

Grape

Color Plate I, *opposite*
Blue hydrangeas and purple-red asters in a Hogarth curve make an effective display to decorate the summer altar.

Color Plate II
Mrs. Raymond A. Carter of Pound Ridge, New York, uses oats, juniper, and vivid chrysanthemums for a Thanksgiving church arrangement. The centerpiece is made from fruits attached with florists' picks to a large cabbage impaled on a pin holder.

Color Plate III
Flowers in tall pedestal vases and simple pew decorations set the stage for an elegant church wedding.

up; in the evening it is cut down, and withereth." There are many references in the Bible to grass.

Holly—Stands for Christ's crown of thorns; *Ilex aquifolium* is closely associated with Christmas tradition.

Hyacinth—The hyacinth of Greek youth may have been iris. Symbolizes power, prudence, and peace of mind in Christian tradition. It grew in Solomon's garden.

Hyssop—Some refer to it as a reed, but most authorities believe it is a mint, *Origanum vulgare,* or pot marjoram. Symbol of cleanliness and freshness. John 19:29 refers to vinegar put on reed to moisten Jesus' lips on the cross.

Iris—The lily of antiquity is known today as the iris. Iris in Greek mythology was the goddess of the rainbow; in fact the name comes from Greek word for rainbow. The flower represents the passion of Christ in Church use. St. Peter's Roman Catholic Church combines the rose, the lily, and the iris in its altar frontals.

Ivy—Represents fidelity and eternity. Greeks and Romans made garlands of ivy and roses for those who excelled in sports and bravery. *Hedera helix* was sacred to Bacchus; hence "the Jews were compelled to go in procession to Bacchus, carrying ivy"— 2 Maccabees 6:1.

Jasmine—Its attributes of grace and elegance cause it to be sometimes associated with the Virgin Mary.

Juniper—The Algum tree of the Bible.

Laurel (Sweet or Bay)—Represents triumph and eternity. See Psalm 37:35. Also used as a reward for victory according to oriental folklore.

Lilies—See Iris.

Lilies (Lilium chalcedonicum)—Scarlet lily referred to in the Song of Solomon 5:31.

Lilium (Candidum)—See Madonna Lily.

Lily of the Valley—Symbol of humility, much used in religious paint-

Holly   Lily of the Valley

ings. Some translations from Hebrew named this as the flower intended as lilies of the field, but see Anemone.

Lotus—Egyptian lotus is a water lily sacred from remote time. It is the most revered flower of the Japanese.

Madonna Lily (Lilium candidum)—Signifies in sacred art the virginity of Mary, the Mother of Jesus. It is also a symbol of the Resurrection because the lily has the power to reproduce itself. When the bulb is placed in the ground it produces a new bulb, stems and flowers, in which the process of death and new life are inseparable; thus symbolic of immortality though the body perishes.

Magnolia—In Chinese legends it is one of the three most loved of all flowers. Stands for power and pride. Magnolia Stellata may be used as star symbol.

Melon—Watermelon is well known in ancient (and modern) Egypt; the children of Israel wept for it, which kindled the anger of the Lord. See Numbers 11:5.

Mustard Seed—A symbol of creative faith. (Matthew 17:20) i.e. Faith as tiny as a mustard seed can move a mountain.

Myrtle—In ancient Greece, wreaths were made from this shrub and presented to victors in sports, etc., signifies Messianic promises.

Narcissus—Some translators say that meadow-saffron was the Bible's "narcissus;" others prefer the rose. However, narcissus is an old world plant which signifies vanity or self-love, from Greek mythology.

Oak—A long time symbol of strength and endurance, sacred to the Druids. An accepted new meaning is forgiveness and eternity; the branches are seen as uplifted to heaven in prayer.

Oil tree—References in Isaiah are presumed to mean *Elaeagnus angustifolia*.

Oleander—Rosebar or common oleander is an Old World evergreen. See Eccles. 39:13. Symbolizes danger because it is poison.

Olive branch—A symbol of peace from pre-Christian times. The dove brought an olive branch to Noah after the deluge.

Orange—One of the oldest cultivated fruits, it represents the world.

Orchid—Love, beauty, and nobility.

Palm—Victory and eternal peace. In early Grecian and Roman history, palms were given to the victors in skill and strength.

Pansy—Since the Renaissance, a sign of remembrance.

Passion Flower—For several centuries, emblematic of Christ's suffer-

Olive Branch Plate 5 Pomegranate

ing, with special meanings for each part of the flower (see Plate 5). The ten petals show the ten apostles who did not deny or betray our Lord. The rays within the flower show the crown of thorns. The five stamens signify the five wounds of Jesus on the Cross. The three styles stand for the nails. The tendrils stand for the cords with which our Lord was bound, and the leaf stands for a spear.

Peach Blossom—Long life. Cultivated for thousands of years before Christ, the peach blossom through folklore and tradition has come to symbolize longevity.

Pear—Human heart; in religious paintings the pear is often used instead of the apple to represent the fruit of the tree of knowledge of good and evil.

Peony—Long venerated in the Orient, where it is a symbol of wealth, prosperity, and rank.

Pine—The most revered and distinguished of all trees in China. It is associated in folklore with the crane, the most revered bird, and is a symbol of faithfulness.

Plum—Longevity, friendship. It blooms early, and lasts many weeks; branches are popular for winter arrangements in the Orient.

Poinsettia—Represents fertility and eternity; it is a symbol of Christmas festival.

Pomegranate—Its fruit alludes to the fertility of the Christian Church, because of its many seeds, its flower is a symbol of hope and immortality. Bursting pomegranate is sometimes seen as a symbol of resurrection.

Pussy Willow—In England, small sprigs of pussy willow are given to Sunday school children on Palm Sunday.

Reed—See Hyssop.

Rose—A symbol of the promised Messiah. Red rose, symbol of love and martyrdom; white, of purity. (To the early Romans a symbol of victory; to the Greeks, the goddess of love, and in the Christian Church a symbol of love). Official flower for Father's Day arrangements; popular too in Mother's Day designs.

Rose of Sharon—References in the Bible to this blossom are interpreted as meaning the present-day tulip. Sol. 2:1 refers to it to denote Christ's love for the Church.

Shamrock—Holy Trinity.

Spices—Dill, coriander, cumin, mint, mustard, rue, saffron (crocus).

Strawberry—Righteousness and good works.

Thistle—Symbolizes fall of man and has a connotation of sorrow and sin. May be used with symbol of redemption as bursting pomegranate.

Thorn—Jerusalem thorn. Mark 15:17 refers to a thorny shrub and not to the crown of thorns plant as we know it. Most thorny branches have come to symbolize grief, trouble.

Tree of Jesus—Refers to genealogy of Christ, ancestors, etc.

Tuberose—This bulbous herb with its white lily-like flower is a member of the family of Amaryllidaceae of Biblical reference.

Vine—Refers to the Church; emblem of Christ. Solomon 2:13 speaks of figs and tender grapes as God's love for the Church. Christ referred to Himself in "I am the vine, ye are the branches . . ."

Violet—Humility, a symbol of modesty and innocence.

Water lily—The "lily work" at the top of Solomon's Temple (I Kings 7:19) was based on *Nymphaea alba* and the Egyptian lotus, *Nilotus*.

Wheat—Symbolizes the bread of the Eucharist. Bounty of earth. Wheat referred to as the staff of life.

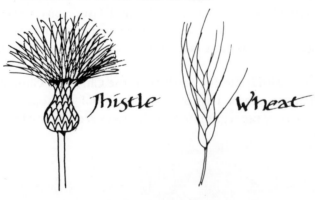

Thistle   Wheat

Willow—Symbolizes the Gospel of Christ because the willow remains whole no matter how many branches are cut; it bends, but never breaks. The willow is especially significant in oriental legends.

Yew—Immortality. Referred to in the Old Testament as a place for resting (under the yew tree) when perplexed or troubled. Sometimes used to mean sorrow.

SYMBOLS OF THE CHRISTIAN YEAR

Associated with every festival and period of the church year are a few distinct and fascinating symbols. Some of the most widely used are listed here.

Advent—Scroll showing in Latin the words of Isaiah's prophecy, "Ecce Virgo concipiet et pariet Filium"—"Behold a Virgin shall conceive and bear a son."
Liturgical color: Violet

Nativity—Glastonbury Thorn, a legendary flower which blooms on Christmas Eve
Liturgical color: White

Epiphany—Five-pointed Star of Bethlehem, which the Wise Men followed to find the promised Messiah
Liturgical color: White
Green (Episcopal)

Lent—Two scourges crossed like an X and resting against a whipping post; any of the symbols mentioned under Lent, Chapter III
Liturgical color: Violet
Black (Good Friday)
White (Holy Saturday)

Advent

Nativity

Lent

Epiphany

Palm Sunday—Palms, which were strewn in Christ's path on his entry into Jerusalem
    Liturgical color: Violet

Maundy Thursday—Chalice, the drinking of the wine at the Lord's Supper

Good Friday—Latin cross and crown of thorns representing the agony of Gethsemane
    Liturgical color: Black

Easter—Bursting pomegranate symbolizing the power of the Lord who burst forth alive from the tomb—rebirth
    Liturgical color: White

Ascension—Fiery chariot depicting the return of Jesus to his Father
    Liturgical color: White

Whitsundy or Pentecost—Paraclete, the tongues of fire representing the Holy Spirit
    Liturgical color: Red

Trinity Sunday—Three fishes, secret symbol of the early Christians referring to the Trinity
    Liturgical color: White
          Green for the season

Palm Sunday

Maundy Thursday

Good Friday

Easter

Ascension

Whitsunday

Trinity Sunday

SYMBOLISM OF LINE AND SHAPE—SACRED AND PSYCHOLOGICAL

Graphic symbolism deals with any form of visual representation including drawing, engraving, etching, diagram, plan, or three-dimensional extension. It is infinite in variety, and every symbol has myriad definitions.

The symbolism in lines and shapes (a series of lines which change direction become shapes) can be applied to enrich church ornamentation; it has been widely used in secular flower arrangements too. Let us consider, for example, the curved line and its possibilities.

Concavities are said to indicate hardship or emptiness; on the other hand, convexities stand for fullness and maturity. The deeply curved line connotes exuberance and abundance and sometimes signifies force if the line direction changes rapidly. The shallow curved line is passive, soft, and flexible, suggesting grace or tenderness.

The crescent is associated with the glory of the Virgin Mary and the new moon, therefore with femininity, as, for example, in the horizontal crescent (Plate 6) representing tranquility, grace, and calm. But there are modifying factors, such as the direction of the crescent. For example, a vertical crescent connotes thrust with flexibility and is therefore well-suited to designs in which a feeling of strength should be projected, as in the case of Plate 7, an arrangement form which could be made to honor Father at home or in the church.

Crescent

Plate 6

Plate 7

The spiral, exemplified in Plate 8, is associated with mystery and complexity, expectancy and escape from the material into the beyond. This is a good form to use for Christian events in which such a mood should be projected, for example, for Ascension Day.

The parabolic curve, which is popular with modern flower arrangers, suggests power, force, and action. In respect to these qualities, it has some similarity to the diagonal.

The diagonal (Plate 9) is transitional, suggesting movement and dynamism. Because diagonals are full of action, danger, uncertainty, and insecurity, they typify our modern age and are the most widely used of all designs in modern art. But diagonals are not the exclusive discovery of modern artists. They have been used throughout the long history of art. Many of Michelangelo's magnificent decorations in the Sistine Chapel are based on diagonals, as was Rubens' *Samson Wrestling with the Lions*—This list could be endless, for the diagonal has prevailed wherever dynamic action has been portrayed.

Radiating lines, on the other hand, which develop uniformly around a central axis (Plate 10) always bring a sense of order and unity. This design, perhaps one of the most basic in nature (snowflakes are one example) is widely used in religious art to suggest radiance, illumination, joy, unity, love and hope from one source. Radiating designs are always appropriate in altar arrangements.

Horizontals are more or less straight lines which symbolize repose, calm and security . . . the type of design which one thinks of in connection with earth; nature; life flowing evenly, smoothly, and on the same plane.

Verticals, opposite of horizontals, connote aspiration, reaching upward, faith, strength, stability, vigor, and courage. In church art, it signified the oneness of God, or the God-head in general. Plate 11 shows a vertical mass design which is appropriate to modern church architecture. Apart from its symbolic form, it fits into the small area allotted to altar flowers in contemporary buildings.

Zigzag lines differ from radiating lines because they lack a single unifying source or force. Zigzags traditionally suggest disquiet and confusion, the broken patterns of the materialist world.

The angle, on the other hand, differs from the zigzag because it is the meeting of two straight lines. It may symbolize the meeting of the celestial and the terrestrial, the reciprocation between God and the world.

Plate 8

Plate 9

Plate 10

Plate 11

The circle has a broad meaning—it is symbolic of infinity (it is never-ending), the universe, the "All." It connotes continuity, complete-ness, maturity, fulfillment, the eternal belief in God. It is a marriage symbol; also as an orb, it represents the world. Coupled with a cross, it becomes an Epiphany symbol. In Plate 12, the theme of circles within circles is used as a Mother's Day design. On a far more magnificent scale, Raphael's *Madonna of the Chair* is organized around this same theme. Circles are an old-time symbol of maternity.

The oval also represents the idea of completeness and continuity. It is an extension of the circle and takes on some of its qualities, while being more interesting and varied.

The fan, which is partly radial, is suggestive of happiness, and when the fan is the folding type it is symbolic of imagination, change, and femininity.

The pyramid suggests strength and composure and some feeling of aspiration.

The equilateral triangle in religious art represents the Trinity. (An aside here might have some interest to flower arrangers. In orien-tal philosophy, the asymmetrical triangle symbolizes the union of heaven-man-earth, or man with nature. When the triangle stands on its base, it represents the female, fixed on earth but aspiring to heaven; inverted on its apex, the uneven triangle represents the male—or naturally celestial—element.)

The square—a static symbol, is the Christian emblem for the unwaver-ing firmness of the church.

The rectangle suggests strength and dependability and is more inter-esting than the square because it offers variety.

There are other factors affecting the symbolism of line. For example, lines have measurement; that is, they are long or short, thick or thin. They may be continuous or broken, two-dimensional as in the embroidery of an altar cloth or three-dimensional as in the branch used in an arrangement. There are lines in plant material which may be called calligraphic, free-hand, and flowing, seeming to be personal and variable. Other lines, as in bent reeds widely used in floral art, seem mechanical, formal, and impersonal. The lines of branches may be firm or wavering, soft or sharp, powerful, agitated, weak, bold, etc. Knowing the symbolism of line will help the designer in any medium to convey the mood or quality that best serves his or her purpose.

Plate 12

COLOR SYMBOLISM

Color symbolism, one of the most universal of all vocabularies, was in use thousands of years before Christ. Colors were a means of denoting rank, marking birth, death and marriage, and showing the position of the heavenly spheres. The colors were plain and the palette was limited to a simple red, blue, yellow, green and purple, but everyone understood their meaning.

Since those early ages, the language of color has become elaborate and highly complicated. For example, it is no longer enough to describe a color as "yellow." One must know whether it is light or dark (its value), whether it is weak or strong (its chroma or intensity) and its position on the color wheel (is it a yellow-blue, yellow-red, etc.) For centuries, artists have explored the mysteries of color as a design element—the most compelling of all the elements perhaps—to evoke a mood and establish a basic atmosphere. It is no accident, for example, that Piero della Francesca painted his Nativity (National Gallery, London) in delicate light pastels, for it was his purpose to achieve a delicate and poetic imagery. But El Greco's nativity scene (*The Adoration of the Shepherds,* Metropolitan Museum of Art, New York) is mystical and supernatural, the canvas heavy with dark and shadowed color values, to which the lighter tones make startling contrast.

Our choice of flowers for important occasions reflects color symbolism. The two colors most frequently used in bridal bouquets are white and red, the white of the pure virginal bride and the red for love. (One remembers Song of Songs, 5:10—My beloved is white and ruddy.) And the union of the lily and the rose through Christian art—in paintings, tapestries, and polychrome wood carvings—mark this color symbolism.

Warm colors—Reminiscent of sun, fire and activity, stimulating and cheering: red, red-yellow, yellow-red, yellow, red-purple.

Cool colors—Quiet, soothing, poised and remote, associated with water, sky and distant mountains: purple-blue or violet, blue, blue-green, and green-blue.

Advancing colors—For actual physical reasons having to do with the way the lens of our eyes adjust to them, some colors make objects seem closer and therefore larger. All reds and related colors such as orange have this quality.

Receding colors—Blues and blue-green make objects seem further away, therefore smaller.

Normal colors—Purple and yellow do not cause any change in eye focus, and are therefore "stay put" colors.

Light

Earlier we mentioned the different effects achieved by della Francesca and El Greco, pointing out that the former used a light key, with not too much contrast in color values, and the latter used a dark key, with strong contrasts in values. In all design, including composition of arrangements, it is important to understand the different effects that can be achieved according to the values you use. Just keep in mind that bright natural light makes one feel cheerful, active and optimistic, twilight makes one thoughtful and introspective, darkness leaves us melancholic and depressed. To create a composition for a happy joyous time, use material which has more of the white than the black value; penitential seasons can have a middle or grayed value; mournful ones can be prevailingly dark.

Liturgical and Non-Liturgical Colors

The use of certain colors as "correct" in liturgy is of comparatively recent vintage, and is by no means universally accepted. For example, although white is the typical color for Easter, red is chosen in some of the Anglican churches and green in some of the French ones. Many churches have disapproved of the trend towards special colors, and others—either through lack of knowledge, lack of interest, or lack of funds—have elected to choose one color which best fits the architecture of their church and use it the year round.

Nevertheless, since the trend is towards more liturgy, rather than less, we have indicated the colors which have the greatest general acceptance. Obviously the palette of liturgical colors is limited to white, violet, green, red and black.

In churches which continue to be non-liturgical, the color range is greater, but still circumscribed, quite often, by the wishes of local clergymen, who should be consulted whenever the need arises.

White symbolizes purity, innocence, divinity, joy and victory. White paraments, the clothing of angels, saints and Christ glorified, are used during Christmas, Epiphany, Easter and on Trinity Sunday. White is emblematic of the states of illumination, ascension, revelation, and pardon.

Violet symbolizes the majesty of Christ in His humility and the penitence of Saints. It is the liturgical color for Lent and Advent. It has a subdued, solemn and melancholy quality.

Purple, the imperial color of ancient Rome always associated with royalty, is much more intense than violet and represents qualities such as power, wealth, and majesty. Both violet and purple are bridges between red and blue and have some of the attributes of each.

Red is the symbol of zeal, courage, love, and aggressiveness. It also represents wine, blood, and fire for the martyrs who died for their Christian faith. It is used for the seasons of Pentecost, Reformation, and the lesser festivals of the church, such as the marriage ceremony, Thanksgiving, Fourth of July, Mother's Day, etc.

Blue is cool, aloof, and serene, a spiritual color which in ecclesiastical use symbolizes faith, hope, serenity, and fidelity. Although not a liturgical color, it is associated with the Virgin Mary in many religious paintings. A deep blue sometimes has an association with royalty. Blue is accepted at most seasons; often when the minister plans to preach on faith, the altar guild uses blue.

Yellow, representing splendor and illumination, the symbol of the sun in religious art, is used at weddings and included at fall festivals to suggest happiness and fulfillment. But while clear yellow, the symbol for the sun, is translated in religious paintings and vestments of the church as gold and gold leaf, it is also the emblem (darkened, greened, and neutralized) of treachery, and Judas has often been painted wearing yellow garments.

Gold is a favorite at weddings, at Christmas, and during Advent. It is associated with solemnity, dignity, richness, and power. When used with purple, it connotes the royalty of kings and queens. Also signifies fruits of the spirit, illumination, and the sun. Values are modified depending on the kind of gold shown—a bright gold is youthful, a bronze gold connotes antiquity, etc.

Silver, used often at Easter in the crescent form, it represents the moon, evening, and change and maturation.

Green, symbol of eternal life and hope, and the color most prominent in Nature, signifies growth. It is used in liturgical churches from Epiphany to pre-Lent, and again after Trinity Sunday to Advent. Jealousy or hypocrisy may also be a connotation as Jeremiah refers to faces changing color and becoming yellowish-green (livid).

Orange suggests gaiety and fire or flames. Thus, for example, it is used to suggest the flames of the fiery chariot, a symbol for Ascension Day.

Brown and *ochre* are symbolic colors for the earth and may be used appropriately for Thanksgiving and Labor Day.

Black symbolizes death, darkness, and evil. Black for mourning and penitence is a very old tradition, and on Good Friday black is often draped over the cross.

SYMBOLISM OF THE CROSSES

There are more than four hundred variations of the cross, a symbol which existed before Christianity. It has myriad complex meanings, but two are primary—the historical one of the crucifixion or of "suffering on the cross" and the more abstract meaning of agony. Because the cross-piece cuts cleanly across the upright it stands for the conjunction of opposites, wedding the spiritual with the physical.

Of the many crosses that appear in the visual history of Christianity —in architecture, applied decoration, altar fittings, sculpture and painting—space permits discussion of only a few, those which most pertain to our present day worship.

Anchor Cross—Cross of the Catacombs, one of the most interesting crosses in history. The persecuted Christians, holding their worship services in the Catacombs beneath Rome, wanted a religious symbol whose significance would be hidden, the Cross in its original form being too bold to use. As a disguise, they adopted the anchor which was the sign of the fisherman but also contained the cross bar. Symbolically, the anchor means life eternal, and the Cross, Salvation. This is The *Crux Dissimulata*—The Cross that is not a Cross.

Calvary Cross—The Graded or Calvary Cross is a favorite. It is the Latin Cross on three steps or grades, symbolizing, in descending order, faith, hope, and love.

Celtic, or Irish Wayside Cross—Also known as St. Martin's Cross and
the Iona Cross, and is used by the Congregational and Episcopal
churches. It takes its name from an actual red granite carved
cross standing before the Cathedral of Iona, on the "Isle of
Saints" off the West Coast of Scotland. Although there is variety
among the Celtic Crosses themselves, the St. Martin's Cross is
considered one of the finest examples. It has a ring or halo around
the crossing, falling just inside the short arms representing life
eternal or the Resurrection. It is noted for its carved designs.

Cross and Crown in Jewels—The emblem of the Cross and Crown is
often used in vestments or Bible markers. The Cross symbolizes
the faithful who have suffered hardships, persecution, and death,
and the Crown is their reward of eternal life (see Plate 13).

Cross Fleur-DeLis—A .Greek Cross with four arms terminating in
three-fold design. A beautiful design with a fleur-de-lis at each
termination.

Greek Cross—The Greek Cross, with its symmetrical arms, symbolizes
the perfect balance and simplicity that the Greeks demanded in
literature, art, even physical culture.

Latin Cross—Perhaps the most famous, most revered, and most employed by the Protestant churches. It appears frequently as the
actual cross upon which Christ was crucified. It is often seen
with a scroll attached to the top of the cross on which the letters
I.N.R.I. are written. The letters indicate the Latin inscription,
Iesus Nazarenus Rex Iudaeorum—Jesus of Nazareth, King of the
Jews. This inscription is shown in accordance with John 12:19-22

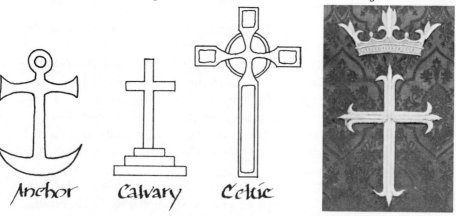

Anchor   Calvary   Celtic

—"Pilate also wrote a title and put it on the cross; it read 'Jesus of Nazareth, the King of the Jews.'" The Latin Cross appears many times in photographs shown in this volume.

St. Peter's Cross—At St. Peter's request, he was crucified in an inverted position, so the Cross on St. Peter's symbol is upside down, and the keys represent the Keys to the Kingdom of Heaven.

Triumph Cross—The Cross of Victory and Conquest. A Latin Cross on a globe symbolizing conquest of the world by Christianity. A favorite in stained glass windows. Religious paintings often shown Christ holding this symbol.

Trinity Cross—This rather elaborate and beautiful cross has three fleur-de-lis at each arm. Appropriate for ecclesiastical embroidery on Church hangings for the Trinity season.

A GLOSSARY OF BIBLICAL OBJECTS AND THEIR SYMBOLISM

You can add a new dimension to your hobby, whether it involves mosaics, pottery, enamel work, or needlecraft. Embroider the symbols on banners and paraments; include them as accessories in your floral designs; incise them into clay containers. You can also use Biblical objects as points of departure for writing flower-show themes. For example, a quotation mentioning "pitch" could be the inspiration for an arrangement with coal as an accessory, or in black and white. Be sure, however, to explain the symbolism in every way possible.

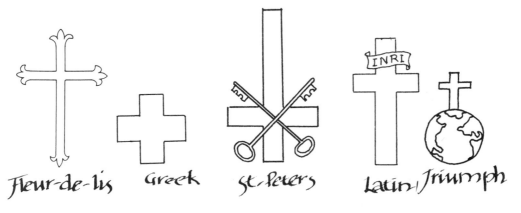

Fleur-de-lis   Greek   St. Peters   Latin/Triumph

Alpha and Omega—The first and last letters of the Greek alphabet, alpha and omega symbolize the beginning and the end. Their usage as a symbol comes from Revelation 22:13—"I am the alpha and omega, the first and the last, the beginning and the end."

    with anchor—Symbolizes eternal hope (see Plate 14).

    with Chi Rho and crossed lines—Chi Rho (Christ is Eternal) and two sets of three intertwining lines cross, and signify the Trinity. Together they form a symbol that is appropriate for use during the Trinity season (see Plate 15).

    with Chi Rho and wheat—Christ is eternal, the beginning and end of all things, the "bread of life" (see Plate 16).

Anchor—Hope, "Like an anchor of the soul, sure and steadfast," 2 Heb. 6.19, has caused the anchor to be used as symbol of Christian hope, particularly when used in anchor cross. The anchor was used by early Christians possibly because cross bar looked like a cross.

Ark (of the Covenant)—A sacred wooden chest inlaid with gold, it was guarded by ancient Hebrews who carried it into battle, considering it representative of God. In Christianity, its basic symbolism is that the essence of spiritual and physical life can be contained in a minute container until conditions are right for a rebirth or re-emergence and diffusion. Therefore, symbolically, the Church holds all that is most basic to our lives.

Arrow—The word of God, sharp and powerful.

Ashes—Penitence—Ashes from palms of Palm Sunday (also represent fleeting things).

Basket—Wicker baskets were common in ancient Palestine, and are referred to in the Bible in connection with miracle of the loaves, carrying Moses, etc. They could be used for symbolic value as container for flower arrangements.

Boat—The Church.

Bread—The Lord's broken body—also symbolized by wheat, as the

Plate 14   Plate 15

Plate 16

Candelabra

breaking of bread in the Last Supper, a Communion symbol.

Candle—Light of the world. One candle stands for Christ; three candles stand for the Holy Trinity; five candles stand for the wounds of Christ; six candles stand for the six days of creation; seven candles stand for the gifts of the Holy Spirit. A lighted candle proclaims that Christ is the "Light of the World."

Candlestick or Candelabra—Two-branched or two candles = the Lord's two-fold nature, human and divine. Seven-branched = Jewish faith or hope. Seven golden candlesticks = seven churches (Rev. 1:12, 20) Candlesticks are sometimes seen as framed by olive trees—Zech 4.1-14.

Christmon—A monogram representing Christ. A symbol seen in many church windows and engraved upon the wood of pulpits and baptismal fonts.

Coral—When used with Christ Child means protection against evil. The word comes from the Hebrew for pebble or small stone (Job 28:18).

Cornucopia—Abundance.

Crosier staff—Authority.

Crown of thorns—Christ's suffering.

Crowns—Referred to repeatedly in Bible, symbol of glory, victory, power, prosperity, etc. Three crowns are used at Epiphany to symbolize the Wise Men.

Cup—Gethsemane, often coupled with the Passion Cup.

Cupid—Love

Dawn—Dawn of eternal salvation—overcoming sin, symbol of Advent.

East—Sunrise, symbol of Christ, the Sun of the Universe.

Emerald—In ancient times, this name was general for any grass-green stones. See Exodus 28:17; Revelations 21:19.

Fire—Fervor of saints and Christians, particularly used for Pentecost. Also a mark of His presence.

Fisherman—Baptism.

Flame—Voice of God.

Fleur-De-Lis—A motif of great antiquity. Said to have been drawn from the lily or iris, it appeared in gold against a blue field on early French shields, as an emblem of royalty. Stands in Church symbolism for the Trinity and is used in a three-fold design on the Greek cross.

Fountain—"The fountain of living waters" metaphor for God (Jeremiah 2, 13).

Fringes—Jesus wore a garment with fringes which the sick tried to touch, thinking it had powers to cure disease. Hence could be used symbolically as arrangement accessory.

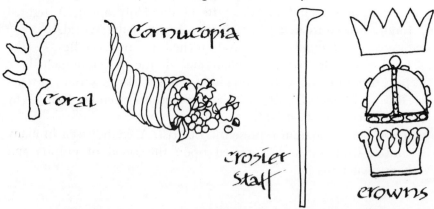

Garden—Globe encircled by serpent—fall of man.

Gold—Pure light, heavenly element in which God lives.

Halo—Divine light.

Hand—The hand of God—a symbol used pointing downward, surrounded by flames to show that the hand of God is over the souls of the righteous. All-Saints' Day symbol. "Laying on of hands"—Blessing, healing, the gift of the Holy Spirit.

Harbor—Eternal life.

Heart—Charity.

Helmet—Paul refers to helmet "And an helmet of salvation upon his head."—Isaiah 59:17. Salvation.

Hill—From the Scriptures—referring to Jesus, as well as the Church, set in a city built on a hill, that cannot be hidden.

House on a Rock—From the Scriptural admonition that if you build a house on sand, calamity will come; it will be washed away; but our church is permanent and everlasting because it is built on a solid foundation.

IHS—Monogram of Jesus.

crowns of thorns

cupid

IHS

Dawn

fleur-de-lis

Hand

Iron—References in Bible use iron to symbolize solidity.

Key—Symbol of authority. Jesus spoke of the "Key of Knowledge"—
of God and his salvation.

Lamp—Word of God; symbolic of Christian knowledge.

Light—Symbol of Christ as in John 8:12, "I am the light."

Lyre—Concord; amity.

Moon, Crescent—Virgin.

Nails—Christ's suffering. Usually three nails are shown.

Necklace—Symbol of wisdom, pride, beauty.

Nude figure with wings—Time.

Oil—Grace of God.

Pearl—Salvation, most precious stone.

Pillar and cord—Scourging—represent the trial of Jesus.

Pitch—"Black as pitch;" evil, sinful state. Can be interpreted as coal.

Pottery—Simile for human fragility. Also molding of clay (human)
to God's will.

Rainbow—Union and pardon.

Rivers—Tradition; four sacred rivers—the Pison, Gilon, Tigris, and
Euphrates—called the four rivers of Paraclese, flowing from a
single rock represent the four Gospels flowing from Christ.

Rocks—Symbols of the Lord, and of the Church as the foundation of
our beliefs. Comes from the story of Moses, who smote the rock
from which water burst forth, Peter (*petra* = rock) was the name
which Jesus gave to Simon, whose faith is referred to as a rock.

Rope—Symbol of the passion because Christ was bound with rope.

Salt—Strength, superiority, perpetuity. Symbol of hospitality.

Scales—Unbalanced—unjust trial of Jesus; balanced—justice.

Scepter—Symbol of Kingship often referred to in Bible.

Scroll—Wisdom; attributes of Apostles.

Shamrock—Trinity; St. Patrick.

Shell—The scallop shell particularly represents the pilgrimages of the
Aapostles. Also used to symbolize baptism.

Shepherd—Christ.

Shield—Faith. With crescent moon, glory of the Virgin Mary; with
lily, the Annunciation; with rose, promise of the Messiah.

Ship—It is essential to learn to sail the seas of passion to reach the
Mountain of Salvation, or to attain great peace, so that the
Church becomes the Ship of Salvation, sailing the seas.

Signum Dei—A combination of two Greek initials X and P, meaning

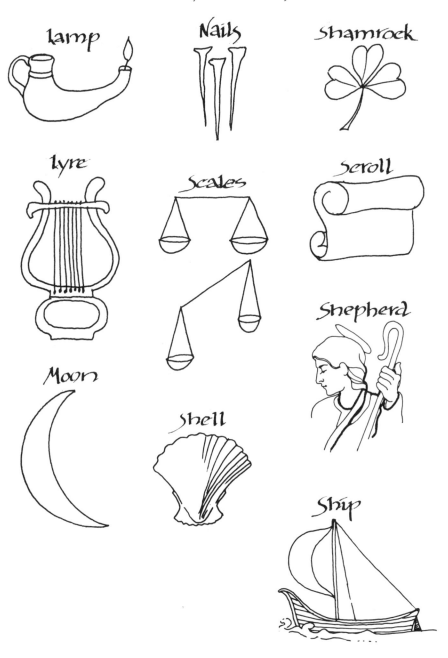

lamp

Nails

Shamrock

lyre

Scales

Scroll

Moon

Shell

Shepherd

Ship

Christ. Said to be a symbol older than the cross. Here the P can be interpreted as the sun shining over the cross, illuminating it. A .contemporary altar design uses the Signum Dei as the central motif in Plate 17. Mrs. John Kestel has composed an asymmetrical arrangement with a dahlia center and podocarpus and aspidistra foliage.

Silver—Purity and charity. Precious metal tested by fire.

Smoke—Vanity; fleetingness of life.

South—Seat of light and warmth, associated with the New Testament, especially Epistles.

Staff—Refuge; strength; God's protection. Also the shepherd's crook is a symbol for the Nativity.

Star—Divine light. Five-pointed = Star of Epiphany or of Virgin Mary; (Mary in Hebrew is Miriam, meaning star). Six-pointed = Star of David or of Creation. Also emblematic of God the Father. Seven-pointed = seven gifts of the Holy Spirit. Eight-pointed = Star of Baptism.

Straw—A thing without value, compared to the sinful which, like straw, will be carried away or consumed by fire.

Sun—Happiness. The sun form is another of the prophetic symbols for Jesus. To identify it as a Christ symbol, a monogram is placed in the center—IHS—Greek for Jesus.

Sword—The penetrating word of God. Also symbolizes martyrdom, or violent death and with the palm, symbolizes the Holy Innocents, martyrs on December 28.

Trefoil—An emblem of the Trinity—the clover—knowledge of the divine essence gained by hard labor.

Triangle—Equilateral, Trinity.

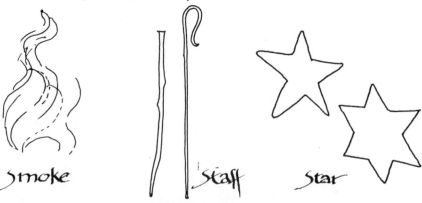

smoke   staff   Star

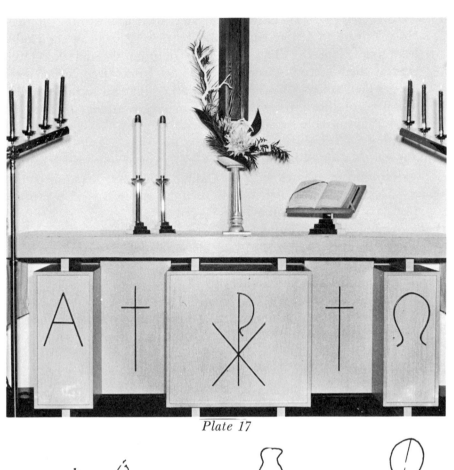

Plate 17

Sun

Sword

Trefoil

Triangle

Trinity Sign (triquetra)—Three equal arcs, used as a symbol of the Holy Trinity to denote equality of the three Persons ·of the Godhead (see Plate 18). The lines run continuously and therefore express their eternal existence. They are interwoven, which expresses their unity. The center forms an equilateral triangle, itself a symbol of the Trinity. Each pair of arcs combines to form a "vesica" or aureole, which is indicative of glory.

Units of three—Trinity.

The Vineyard—Grapes and grape vines are "fruit of the spirit;" hence a vineyard is associated with the Church which nurtures this fruit.

Water—Cleansing and purifying, as used in sacrament of baptism; God is a "spring of living water"—Jer. 2:13.

Well—Symbol of baptism, life, and rebirth; flowing fountains of water. Salvation—life is a pilgrimage, and the well saves the pilgrim.

West—Seat of darkness and abode of evil.

Wine—Christ's blood, shed on the cross.

Wings—Divine mission; symbol of angels, archangels, seraphim archangels, and cherubims. Winged creatures symbolize the four evangelists, Matthew, Mark, Luke, and John.

Wreath—Eternity; (fruit, flowers) cycle of seasons.

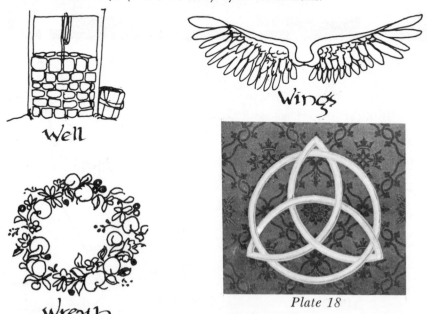

Well

Wings

Wreath

Plate 18

THE FAUNA OF THE BIBLE

Many of these can be used as story-telling accessories in your floral composition. Animals can be shown realistically or in abstraction, for example, peacock feathers to represent the peacock, leopard-print fabric for the leopard, etc. Children especially respond to the appeal of animals. Do not, therefore overlook the opportunity to use figurines in Bible teaching. As with plants of the Bible, exact translations of the Hebrew names for animals, insects and birds are not clearly established, but the following appear to have general acceptance.

Ant—Wisdom and foresight. Prov. 6:6; 30:24.

Bat—Emblem of idol worship—Isaiah 2:26.

Bears—According to Isaiah, they will lie down with cows at the coming of Messiah.

Bee—Means Deborah in Hebrew.

Bird—Variable symbolism. Sometimes stands for a believer in Christ.

Bull—Fertility and power symbol. Bull-worship was common in many religions.

Butterfly—The Resurrection.

Camel or dromedary—See Matthew 19:24, 23:24 and Mark 10:25 for proverbs.

Donkey—Stubborn, steady, surefooted.

Cocks and hens—Resurrection symbols used in many catacomb paintings. The cock anouncing the dawn is compared to proclamation in Christianity of belief in life beyond. The cock is a symbol of watchfulness often used on church steeples.

Crane—Biblical references could mean swallow, as translations are inconclusive. Allusions are to swiftness.

Butterfly

Crocodile—Sacred to Egyptians; the river dragon referred to in Ezekiel 29:3.

Dog—Scavengers. Objects of contempt.

Dolphin—Whales and sea monsters of Biblical reference are presumptively the dolphins. In heraldry and early Christian art, dolphins (or porpoises as they are known to sailors) also represent swiftness, love, diligence; Resurrection symbol too. Plate 19, featuring a dolphin with sea plume, sponge, and a water lily made of shells is an interpretative design: *"And God created great whales, and every living creature that moveth, which the waters brought forth abundantly, after their kind, and every winged fowl after his kind."* Genesis 1:21

Plate 19

Dove—the third person of the Trinity, the Holy Spirit, is commonly represented as a dove, so the spirituality and power of sublimation of the Church is thus symbolized by the dove. A messenger of peace to Noah in the Flood. A baptism symbol. Also "gentle spirit."

Dragon—A universal symbol of Satan; evil.

Eagle—Height or soaring of the spirit; prayer rising swiftly to the Lord. Heraldic eagles could be used. Often mentioned in the Bible and associated with St. John, evangelist.

Fish—A secret sign for believers in Jesus Christ; Lord's Supper; miracle.

Fox—Herod is called one (Luke 13:32).

Frog—Symbol of uncleanliness. (Rev. 16:13).

Gazelle—Gentleness and grace.

Giraffe—Timidity and fleetness.

Goat—Sacrificial Offering. Many Biblical references to it.

Grasshoppers, Crickets, Locusts—Represented Judgment of God.

Hornet—Plague or punishment.

Horse—Symbol of Ascension; it drew the chariot of Jesus.

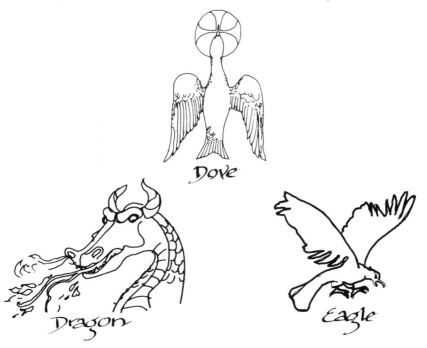

Dove

Dragon

Eagle

Lamb—Symbol of Jesus Christ. The white pennant-of-resurrection banner represents the body of Christ, which is attached to the cruciform staff, representing the cross on which the Lamb of God died and through which the risen Christ saves the world. The lamb shown standing (see Plate 20) suggests that the Lamb of God is triumphant, risen. Some authorities say the Lamb is a symbol because of its humility, others because Christ sacrificed for us and the lamb was the sacrificial animal of ancient Jewry.

Leopard—"And the beast which I saw was like unto a leopard." Rev. 13:2.

Lion—King of beasts, mentioned more than a hundred times in the Bible and with varying significance. Christ was the lion of the tribe of Judah.—(Rev. 5:5.) Devil was likened to a roaring lion. (Peter 5:8.)

Moth—Destruction.

Ostrich—Foolish "God hath deprived her of wisdom"—Job 39:17.

Owl—Bird of good omen.

lion

Plate 20

Color Plate IV, *opposite*
Long spikes of gladioli and snapdragons with chrysanthemums and grapes make a stately design which, with a twin on the opposite side, would be appropriate for most altars.

Peacock—Resurrection. The legend of the peacock was that it did not decay after death, shedding its feathers each year to grow new, more beautiful ones. The eye of the tail represents the "all seeing eye" of the church.

Partridge—Alludes to foolish deceitfulness—"as the partridge sitteth on eggs and hatcheth them not, so he that getteth riches, and not by right, shall leave them in midst of his days, and at his end shall be a fool." Jeremiah 17:11.

Phoenix—Resurrection. After the legendary phoenix has lived five hundred years, its nest is set on fire by the sun. The phoenix is consumed and then rises from the ashes to start life again.

Pig—Symbol of impurity.

Serpent—Devil, Satan, sin, wickedness, temptation.

Snake around rod—Symbol of healing.

Stag—Always praised for its agility and grace.

Stork—Several references in *Bible*. See Psalms 104-7, etc.

Wolves—Signifies ravenous, cruel.

Phoenix   Serpent

Color Plate V, *opposite*
Brilliant garden flowers, mainly in the red family, are designed in a equilateral triangle to honor the Trinity season.

III

Flowers for the Major Events of the Church Year

1. ADVENT—A PERIOD OF EXPECTATION

I shall see him but not now: I shall behold him but not nigh:
There shall come a star out of Jacob, and a Sceptre shall rise
out of Israel. Numbers 24:17

Advent Sunday, the first day of the church year, is a wondrous time of anticipation of Christmas and preparation for the coming of the Redeemer of mankind, but also of penitence and meditation. Fall flowers are gone and the Christmas season is heralded with wreaths and evergreens, but these are not decorated, and arrangements are pure and subdued to fit the spirit of Advent. Flowers and decorations tell the story of Christmas coming.

Liturgical churches use violet to signify penitence and introspection. The change to a frontal of this color on the altar presages the change in mood from Autumn and Thanksgiving which preceded Advent. On the eve of the Nativity, December 24, white is used. Non-liturgical churches use green, as well as white and red, for Advent decorations throughout the season.

Advent is celebrated as the fulfillment of the Old Testament prophecy of the coming of the Messiah. Its meaning is to be found in three ways, all connected with this coming: (1) the coming of Christ in the flesh, the Christmas celebration, (2) His coming in word and spirit, to be meditated upon throughout the Church year and (3) His coming in glory at the end of time.

In the churches during Advent, perhaps the most commonly used decoration is a simple wreath of cedar, pine cones, holly, holly berries, and five candles (see Plate 21). A candle is lighted each Sunday for four Sundays then, on Christmas Eve, a white candle is lighted to represent the coming of Christ. It is placed in the middle of the four burning candles and all five burn throughout the service. The candles symbolize the various aspects of Christ to which mankind looks forward, His Love, His Forgiveness.

Plate 21

In some churches a pair of unadorned Christmas trees is placed in the sanctuary, on either side of the altar, and ball-shaped bay trees in pots may be used in the same way. (These should be kept outdoors in the churchyard or garden during the summer, the shoots pruned back to keep the trees in shape.)

Trinity Methodist Church of Deland, Florida, is shown in Plate 22 with traditional greenery and candles used in Advent celebrations. The walls are pale gray; the wood panelling is dark brown, the rug is bright red. Fresh pine was used around the arch, homemade candles in the choir loft and on the sanctuary. Magnolia foliage with poinsettias and "glamellias" formed the center of interest.

To make homemade candles, melt old candles in a large can over low heat. Beat the melted wax as you would whip cream. Then plaster this wax over cylinders in which candles were previously inserted.

To make "glamellias" for a round center of interest, (spiky gladioli are not suited for use as a focal point), wire together three florets of gladiolus. Press gently open with fingers. Assemble the wired florets around a gladiolus bud, wire and tape stem.

In the home, Advent is a season of close family feeling and happiness, as each member busies himself with buying presents and joins in preparations for festivities and decorations. The lighting of the candles in an Advent wreath is a good time to teach children about the first Christian festival, and Bible verses are selected for memorization and discussion. Selections can be made by subject. Candles, for example, are the subjects in the following verses: Matthew 5:15, Mark 4:21, Luke 8:16, Rev. 18:23, 22:5, and in many of the earlier books.

As Christmas approaches, evergreens can be brought into the house to serve as Advent decorations; though unadorned they bring with them the clear, sharp scent of pine which, like all evergreens, symbolizes eternity. For the eve of the Nativity, a company table is set with a red linen cloth (see Plate 23). A golden urn holds berried foliage and gilded grass with a large white poinsettia. Such an arrangement would be well suited to use in the social hall during the holiday season.

Plate 22

Plate 23

2. CHRISTMAS—A FESTIVAL OF JOY

And the Angel said unto them fear not for behold I bring
you good tidings of great joy which shall be to all people.
For unto you is born this day in the city of David a Savior,
which is Christ the Lord. Luke 2:10-11

Although one tends to think of Christmas as being celebrated with the traditional Christmas colors of red, green, and white, the liturgical color is *white,* and white paraments are used. Red and blue are two exceptions: *red* for December 26th, St. Stephen Martyr's Day, and for December 28th, the day for St. John the Apostle; *blue* is associated with the Madonna.

In non-liturgical practice, the entire church, particularly the sanctuary, takes on the colors of the many flowers and materials associated with the season. Red is used widely. A favorite plant of the season, the poinsettia, like the Christmas rose, is frequently the subject of legends. A sixteenth century tale tells of a little girl who follows the Wise Men to the cradle of the Infant Jesus and weeps because she has no flowers to place beside the manger. An angel appears and bids her to take the weeds she holds to the altar, and as she does so the weeds blossom into a vivid, beautiful poinsettia.

White flowers are used symbolically to represent the purity and innoncence of the new-born Babe, and white roses, lilies, white carnations, etc. carry out this idea in decorating the church.

In the milder climates of our country, the feeling of the first Christmas, which occurred after all in a mild climate, may be captured in the non-liturgical church with palm, magnolia, poinsettias, and other foliage and blossoms of the East; churches in colder climates can create winter wonderlands with the fresh greenery of various evergreens. Decorations for window sills, the front of the pulpit, and other locations in the church can be made of cones, greens, and ribbon to bring joy to the building.

The more contemporary, lighter churches of some communities call for a different treatment at Christmas from the conventional Gothic structures which are so softened and enriched by traditional greenery. Here, the arranger has an opportunity to employ some of the newer methods in arrangement, using ingenuity and imagination to construct novel designs.

Trinity Methodist Church in DeLand, Florida, was given a glamorous holiday look with a color scheme of red, white, and gold. As shown in Plate 24, the sanctuary and front of the church were treated symmetrically with Christmas trees placed on tall pedestal tables flanking the sanctuary, and matching arrangements of potted red poinsettias dramatized by tall white candles placed on either side of the communion rails. The arrangements on the altar are red and white carnations massed with pittosporum.

Plate 24

Christmas Wreaths

Christmas is a family festival. We celebrate it by making our homes
shiny and bright, singing Christmas carols, providing rich feasts and
giving gifts following the example of the Wise Men of the East. Although many books have been written about Christmas decorations
and thousands of arrangements suitable for this holiday have been
pictured, a few which have a particular symbolism are shown here.

Few Christian homes at Christmas seem truly decorated without a
wreath at the door, in the window, or perhaps as a focus in some
living area other than that in which the Christmas tree is placed. The
round form symbolizes eternity, the flowers and fruits symbolize the
cycle of the seasons.

The Christmas doorway in the home of Mr. and Mrs. Arnold E.
Boedicker of Cuyahoga Falls, Ohio, is of hand-carved heavy oak with
inserts of glass made by the owner to give the effect of stained glass
reminiscent of church window art (see Plate 25). The Della Robbia
wreath and swag are by Mrs. Boedicker.

Luca della Robbia was a medieval sculptor who made glazed pottery
wreaths which are widely used by flower arrangers as inspiration for
holiday decorations. Fruits, nuts, cones, seed pods and other dried or
artificial materials, well proportioned, are wired individually to a
frame of quarter-inch hardware cloth backed with heavy cardboard.
(Some florists sell a pre-made frame.) To wire the nuts, drill a hole
in one end, insert a wire, and twist it. To raise small nuts from the
surface, make them into a bunch by wiring several of them together
before twisting to the frame. The materials used for the wreaths and
swags may be sprayed, painted, or shellacked. The wreath can be
used for years, so it is well worth the initial effort. Fresh greens may
also be used, but their life is limited, of course. To use fresh evergreens, cut them into short lengths of about six inches and wire them
to the frame, overlapping the material so wire does not show.

Plate 25

Another wreath, this one for a table, is made of Japanese yew, small and large red grapes, the gold Christmas balls on a styrofoam circle (see Plate 26). Florist pins were used to hold the materials in place. A lighted oil lamp in the center makes the bright red glass sparkle and gleam.

Madonna Theme

The Madonna and Child theme is rich with meaning for this holiday. Scripture dictates that this motif should be used only at Christmas and not, as many flower arrangers mistakenly do, at Easter. Plate 27 shows a modified crescent line which is formed with English ivy, Christmas roses, and grapes. (The symbolism of the design form and the plant materials is explained in Chapter 2.)

"Devote yourselves to hospitality"—8 Romans 12:13. It is a privilege at Christmas to gather friends and family around our table, and Plate 28 shows a table set for hospitality. Designed by Lucy Staley of Rhinebeck, New York, it features a frosted lighted Madonna figurine by Fostoria, red roses, and babies'-breath. The tablecloth is strewn with printed roses.

Plate 26

Plate 27

Flower Arrangements

Marguerite Bozarth of Seattle, Washington, made the arrangement in Plate 29 for a garden club Christmas show. Branches of evergreen were woven through the candlestick and also used as a base. The candles were red, and red ribbons were shaped into poinsettias.

Plate 30 shows dried white sea fan, a red poinsettia, and blue artificial grapes in a royal blue glass container.

Christmas in Other Countries

From the Wise Men of the East until the present day, there has been a procession of people from all denominations seeking the place where "the young Child lay." Each country has its own traditions and celebrations.

From Austria comes the beautiful custom of using three candles as symbols of the light of Christ and God's gift to man. One candle is lighted on Christmas Eve, one on Christmas day and the last on New Year's Day.

Conditioning Poinsettias

Two or three days before cutting, strip all the leaves above where the cut is going to be made. After cutting, place the stem in sand to stop the bleeding. Submerge completely in water for twenty-four hours to harden. Choose the older stems when possible. They will last for several days, if properly conditioned. The ends may be burnt instead of using the sand. In either case, they must be submerged in water overnight.

Plate 28 opposite

Plate 29

Plate 30

Both the home and the church in Sicily devote much time to preparation for Christmas. The building of an altar in each takes precedence over all other activities. On Christmas Eve there is a procession through the town while bells ring in celebration.

In Poland this is a period of expectation, hope, and wonderment. When the first star appears on the 24th of December, the Christmas supper begins. Straw is placed under all plates, mats, and tables. One chair is left vacant for the Holy Child, and a wafer, blessed by the priest, is shared by all.

In Norway, where bells begin to ring early Christmas Eve, a beautiful tradition has been developed. Special foods are set out for birds and animals, since these were the only creatures present at the birth of the Christ Child.

3. EPIPHANY—THE MANIFESTATION OF GOD'S GLORY

Now when Jesus was born in Bethlehem of Judea in the days of Herod the King, behold, there came Wise Men from the East to Jerusalem. Matthew 2:1

Epiphany (the word means manifestation) begins on January 6, Epiphany Day, which is sometimes known as Twelfth Night, Twelfth Day, and Little Christmas and is a day of gift-giving in some countries. Epiphany commemorates the manifestation of Jesus to the Wise Men of the East who, according to tradition, represented the Gentiles ultimately to receive the Gospel.

The Wise Men to whom Jesus was made manifest were told to return to their people and bear witness to the miracle they had seen, and for this reason, the Epiphany season has become a time for stressing the missionary function in some churches. The symbol for this is four Latin crosses arranged so that their bases overlap. The resulting "Cross coverlet" suggests the four corners of the world to which the Gospel is carried.

The Magi are also represented by baskets holding gifts for The Child —gold for Christ's kingly office, frankincense for his priestly one, and myrrh for the prophetic one.

Epiphany is also known as the Feast of Lights and there are many scriptural passages which make this clear as in Isaiah 60:3—"The Gentiles shall come to thy light and kings to the brightness of Thy rising."

Since Jasper, Balthasar and Melchior became in legend not only wise men but kings, symbols such as crowns and scepters are used at Epiphany, as well as symbols of the Wise Men themselves.

Plate 31 shows hand-painted figurines of the Three Kings, used with white chrysanthemum and green yew. Since white is used for one week of Epiphany and green for the remainder of the season, the color scheme was fitting for the design and the religious purpose.

The five-pointed star, known as the Star of Bethlehem or Epiphany,

Plate 31

is also a symbol of the journey of the Magi. "Where is he that is born King of the Jews for we have seen his star in the east and are come to worship him." Matthew 2:2.

4. LENT AND HOLY WEEK—A TIME FOR SOUL-SEARCHING

Search me O God and know my heart; try me, and know my thoughts and see if there be any wicked way in me, and lead me in the way everlasting. Psalms 139:23-24

Lent begins on the seventh Wednesday before Easter, and ends at noon on Holy Saturday, the day before Easter Sunday. The special days of the Holy Week, the last week of Lent, have high spiritual significance. These days are Palm Sunday, Maundy Thursday, Good Friday and Holy Saturday. In liturgical churches, violet is the color of this season of penitence and mourning.

Not all Evangelical churches permit flowers during Lent; the Episcopal church uses no flowers between Ash Wednesday and Good Friday, the Methodist church uses flowers all through Lent except for Palm Sunday, and other Protestant churches adopt other methods.

For Palm Sunday, recognized as the day of Christ's triumphal entry into Jerusalem (Matt. 21:8; Mark 11:8; Luke 19:37; John 12:12), an arrangement by Mrs. B. E. Barrett and Mrs. Betty Neilson is shown in the Episcopal Church of DeLand, Florida (see Plate 32). A fan-shaped design was formed out of embryo palmetto palm. All palms were submerged in water overnight. The dark fronds in the background which had reached maturity were trimmed to the desired size. The palms were folded and stapled together the next morning, and set into Oasis in the inside container.

Plate 32

Another arrangement for Palm Sunday appears in Plate 33. Most churches use green foliage or palms, or a combination. Sago palm forms the line of this symmetrical design. The center of interest is magnolia foliage used to keep the arrangement from becoming too busy—a solid smooth texture was needed and supplied by the glossy magnolia leaves. Churches in which flowers are permitted could use a similar arrangement with tulip lilies at the focal area, Plate 34.

Maundy Thursday, the evening before the Crucifixion, marks the date when the Lord's Supper was instituted. "Maundy" comes from the Latin word, *mandatum,* meaning command, and refers to the new commandment at the Last Supper, when Jesus abjured the disciples to love one another.

A representational portrayal of the Lord's Supper is a dramatic arrangement designed by Mrs. John Kestel, Plate 35. Wheat represented the bread, grapes and a wine bottle represent wine. The three white gardenias are set off by green foliage, and an S-curve of driftwood enhances the design. An abstract church window in the background, and an emptied chalice enhance the drama of the arrangement. Used in other rooms of the church and rectory, such an arrangement carries over the spirit of reverence.

For Palm Sunday green foliage such as palms, magnolia and evergreens are used. Flowers if used on Maundy Thursday should be white. For Good Friday only black drapery may be used to cover the cross.

Many other symbols of the Lenten Season refer to the events of Holy Week. They include symbols of the betrayal such as "the head of Judas" or the "thirty pieces of silver," usually symbolized as a money bag, and the lantern, torches and weapons of the soldiers who searched for Jesus. Christ's suffering is symbolized by the two scourges, the hammer and nails, the "vessel of vinegar and gall," the rope, the ladder, the "ewer and basin," symbolic of Pilate's hand washing, and a crowing cock used specifically in reference to Peter's denial of Jesus. Hyssop (sweet marjoram) may also be meaningful.

A more contemporary symbol of the Passion is the passion flower and, of course, the Latin Cross and "the empty cross" both associated with the Crucifixion.

top left Plate 33
below Plate 34
top right Plate 35

Wheat and grapes have great meaning in Christian arrangements and are referred to many times in the Bible, aside from their relationship to the Last Supper. It would be fitting to use them on the altar or in the home during any Christian festival.

Good Friday, the day of the Crucifixion, is observed by all Protestant churches as a day of mourning. Churches are usually opened for prayer during the day. No paraments or flowers are used on the altars, although black may be used as a drape over the cross.

Since Lent uses violet as the liturgical color, it is well within the symbolism of this season to use the informal table setting shown in Plate 36. White damask cloth is the setting for an arrangement which includes grapes in a violet color and violet candles. The flowers can be any seasonal ones from florist or early garden. Plate 37 shows a simple design featuring the lovely magnolia bloom which, with rhododendron leaves, can be cut from the garden in Spring. It is appropriate in the home any time during the season.

Plate 36

Plate 37

Plate 39

Plate 38

5. EASTER—THE BEAUTY AND THE JOY OF THE RESURRECTION

He is not here, he has risen . . . I, if I be lifted up from the earth, will draw all men unto me. John 12:32

Easter Sunday, the most exalted festival of the Christian Church, is the time when flowers symbolize a radiant faith in the Resurrection. With the Hallelujah Chorus sounding our joy and happiness, we adorn the altar with candles and flowers in great masses. Thus we signify the renewal of hope and faith in the souls of men.

Easter Sunday, which occurs on the first Sunday after the first full moon after the Vernal Equinox, has a fluctuating date sometime between March 22 and April 25. This Paschal season lasts for forty days, ending with Ascension Day. White flowers and altar cloths and vestments are used by most churches.

The name Easter is derived from the Anglo-Saxon spring goddess, Eastre, whose festival coincided with the Spring Equinox. The symbols and decorations used at this time are happy ones. Light, flowers, birds, painted eggs and new clothes, as well as symbols of victory and kinship, all suggest the gladness and triumph of resurrection and immortality.

Perhaps, the most meaningful to the arranger is the lily, lavishly used during the Easter season. Lilies not only bloom at Easter, but its process of growth, the way the bulb appears to decay and then its resurrection at Easter, recapitulate the ideas of life from death, or the attainment of immortality.

Since white is the Easter color, white lilies as well as babies'-breath, white gladiolus and other white flowers are highly appropriate. Three designs planned for church settings at this season are shown in the following plates.

A low triangular line is designed for a church that does not have both a lectern and a pulpit (see Plate 38). Light and airy, its spaces are enhanced by babies'-breath.

Another typical Easter design scheme for a church is illustrated here in Plate 39. Easter, calla lilies and stock are combined with babies'-breath inserted among the large flowers to create a light and airy feeling. A large pinholder covered with a block of Oasis wrapped in aluminum foil, into which the flowers are inserted, are the mechanics.

In Plate 40, a church with a large allowance for flowers displays a series of harmonized arrangements placed on two levels—the arrangements *en masse* also have a design quality, which is important in large churches in which details may be lost if viewed from the rear.

Plate 41 designed by Mrs. Guy Yaste of Pensacola, Florida features white lilies, yucca leaves, and yew in a white ceramic container. It could be used equally well at home or in a church setting.

There is rich symbolism around the celebration of Christ's death and Resurrection. The most famous and most revered of these symbols are the chalice cup and the passion cross, representing His suffering and death. This theme of resurrection is a magnificent one for arrangements to be used throughout the church, as the one shown in Plate 42 designed by Mrs. John Kestel of Waterloo, Iowa. The stone has been rolled from the tomb, and the structural material of driftwood from which the Easter lilies and palm fronds emerge represent "But now is Christ risen from the dead and become the first fruits of them that slept." (I. Corinthians 15:20).

Many of the Lenten symbols, visual renderings of the events leading to the Crucifixion, may be used effectively at Easter, for example, the crown of thorns and three nails.

For reasons discussed in Chapter 2, the passion flower is associated with the death and resurrection of Christ, and Plate 43 shows it as a representation of the passion of Christ in a design appropriate for a modern church.

Easter at home

At home, in the excitement of new outfits for the family, Easter gift-giving, egg decorations, and baskets filled with colorful eggs, the emphasis is usually rather remote from the exalted feeling of the church at Easter. But Easter was originally a Spring festival, so do not overlook the opportunities to capture the mood of the season with bright daffodils and simple arrangements of flowers from the garden.

On a more formal plane, the design in Plate 44 of yellow roses and peacock accessories—peacocks are resurrection symbols—is appropriate for the table set for Easter dinner.

In the colder climates, flowers for Easter can be a problem if Easter comes early. Some foresight will bring returns if you cut forsythia, fruit tree branches and other Spring flowers to force them to bloom

Plate 40

Plate 41

Plate 42

Plate 43

early indoors. If Easter lily leaves can be purchased they are helpful with the lilies, but if not, laurel leaves are frequently suggested. Daffodils and tulips are apt to be in bloom and are a welcome sight in church rooms and at home.

Plant symbolism for Easter has been discussed in the preceding pages, but do not overlook animals and insects appropriate to the season. Children always relate to figurines of animals, which can be the basis for Bible talks at any time of year. Some of the best known symbols of the season are the butterfly, cock, hen, dolphin (in Greek mythology this mammal was said to transport the souls of the dead to the land of the blest, hence the dolphin was a resurrection symbol in early Christian history), the eagle, the lamb, the swallow, and the pelican (it loved its young so dearly that it pecked open its own breast to nourish them), and the legendary phoenix.

Plate 44

6. ASCENSIONTIDE—A GREAT FESTIVAL

Nevertheless, I tell you the truth. It is expedient for you that I go away, for if I go not away, the Comforter will not come unto you; but if I depart, I will send Him unto you. John 16:7

Ascension Day, the fortieth day after Easter Sunday, one of the great festivals of the church, should be celebrated with flowers. Beginning always on Thursdays, which is Ascension Day, the season lasts for ten days. Ascension marks the end of Christ's earthly ministry and his return to God the Father. It must have been a very solemn and impressive moment for His followers when he told them that He must depart.

White is the liturgical color of the season and white flowers customarily decorate the church on this occasion, among them calla and Madonna lilies, irises, camellias, white tulips and tuberoses, lilac, peonies, hyacinths and rhododendrons. But many other kinds of white flowers from the provision available in our gardens can be used.

The symbols of the Ascension are the eagle and the fiery chariot, both of which represent the actual passage of Christ to the heavens. The chariot also symbolizes Elijah's ascent as described in 2 Kings 2:11—"And as they still went on and talked, behold a chariot of fire and horses of fire separated the two of them. And Elijah went up by a whirlwind into heaven."

More abstract representations of Ascension can be used in flower arrangements, for the symbolism of Ascension pertains to the inner life, which concerns the upward impulse rather than any actual ascent. All symbols such as the mountain, the ladder, tree, cross, rope and spear representing height and upward thrusting are thus symbols of Ascension.

In a modern church, an altar arrangement (Plate 45) forms a decided triangle against a rose brick wall. It was made by Marguerite Bozarth of the North End Flower Club of Seattle for the Bethel Presbyterian Church, and demonstrates how an essentially traditional and simple bouquet can contribute to an orderly arrangement in an orderly pattern in a contemporary setting. This church has walls of a pale aqua tone, and the carpets are a complementary green. The brass containers, cross and candlesticks are of a heavy matching design. The garden flowers and foliage, predominantly white and green, were

Plate 45

cimicifuga, phlox, petunias, Shasta daisies, snapdragons, nicotiana, iris pods and hosta foliage.

Ascension for the Home

The inspiring message of The Ascension, that He was received into Heavenly places, and that they that do His commandments "may have right to the tree of life, and may enter in through the gates into the city" (Rev. 22:14) lends itself to many arrangements of diverse nature in the home. These may have a simple vertical, upward line suggesting a lifting of thoughts heavenward, as in Plate 46, which uses mainly gladioli, snapdragons, and an echeveria rosette, or the design can be based on the spiral, with all its connotations of mystery and complexity. In Plate 47, bleached whisteria vine spirals around wood roses, which, like the fresh ones, are symbols of love and majesty. The abstract container with its many openings was made for me by Mrs. Stell Phillips of Ocala, Florida.

Plate 48 shows a figurine of Christ used with reverence and dignity. Weathered wood suggests the past, the open flowers (yellow rose and day lily) the present, the buds the future. Dark red grapes are associated with the passion of Christ. The blue of the delphiniums symbolizes faith.

Plate 46   Plate 47

Plate 48

7. WHITSUNTIDE OR PENTECOST—FILLED WITH HOLY SPIRIT

> *Suddenly there came from the sky a noise like that of a strong driving wind, which filled the whole house where they were sitting. And there appeared to them tongues like that of flames of fire, dispersed among them and resting on each one, and they were all filled with the Holy Spirit, and began to talk in other tongues, as the spirit gave them power of utterance.* Acts 2:1-4

Pentecost, meaning fiftieth, occurs fifty days after Easter. It commemorates the day that disciples received the Holy Ghost and the power to speak in different languages. It is also the birthday of the Christian church.

In ancient times, converts wearing white robes were baptized on Sunday during this period, and from their white robes came the name Whitsunday—and Whitsuntide—which some churches still use. There is also conjecture that the name came from the old Anglo-Saxon word "wit" meaning wisdom, an allusion to the outpouring of the spirit of wisdom (Ephesians 1:17). This association of Pentecost with wisdom seems to have some relationship to the Jewish feast of Pentecost or *Shabuot,* which celebrates the anniversary of the giving of the Ten Commandments as well as the grain.

Both liturgical and non-liturgical churches feature red for the eight days of Pentecost. Since red often disappears visually into the darkness of the Sanctuary and against the red frontal used on the altar, it often helps to mix the red with pink or magenta to cut up the color and enable it to be better projected. Of course, the architecture and lighting of the church affect this; in a modern large-windowed church such a problem would not prevail.

Placed on a marble slab to signify the table of stone given Moses, the arrangement shown in Plate 49 may be used at home, on the altar, or in a Gothic or modern church to symbolize the Pentecost. In ancient use, the ten fingers of the hand were related to the Ten Commandments so the symbolism of the "Praying Hands" refers to the giving of the Law.

The Pentecost season which extends to Trinity and summer brings the flowers of the garden into the house in formal and informal arrangements which convey the spirit of worship. Red poppies, pyre-

Plate 49

thrums and peonies might be available from the garden.

A predominantly red design for the home in Plate 50 uses pink hydrangeas, red-violet celosia, and red-orange tuberous begonias with Oregon spruce. The diagonal line has a forward movement. Textural contrast was achieved with the smoothness of the Japanese lamp used as a container.

There is much latitude for garden club or home arrangements at this season. Interpretive arrangements in a more modern mood can convey the drama of the coming of the Holy Spirit.

For example, "And there appeared to them tongues like that of flames of fire . . . and they were filled with the Holy Spirit." This is illustrated in Plate 51, an interpretative design. The black plastic makes a realistic background for the "flames," which are dried traveler's palm, painted orange-red, and the deep red amaryllis so appropriate to Whitsunday.

The descent of the Holy Ghost at Pentecost has been represented in El Greco's famous religious painting "The Pentecost" (Prado Museum, Madrid). With this picture in mind, I planned a flower arrangement (Plate 52), using as my materials a dove, red roses, tuberoses, and ovals made from plastic tubings.

Since the Pentecost season celebrates the birth of the church, flower shows at this season could feature arrangements interpreting the theme. One such design is shown in Plate 53, inspired by the following quotation:

> After this I will return, and will build again the tabernacle of David, which is fallen down; and I will build again the ruins thereof, and I will set it up. Acts 15:16

Since pine is particularly symbolic of the Church (see Chapter 2) I represented the falling down of the old tabernacle with pine roots, inverted, distorted, and painted black. I then added roses as a symbol of Messianic promise in Isaiah 35:1 referring to the rebuilding of the Church.

Plate 50

Plate 51   *Plate 52*

Plate 53

8. TRINITY SEASON—PROCLAIMING THE THREE-FOLD NATURE OF GOD

As thou hast sent me into the world, even so have I sent them into the world. John 17:18

Trinity Sunday follows Pentecost or Whitsuntide in the Christian year, and is observed in honor of the Holy Trinity. It marks the beginning of the second part of the church year, and is a proclamation of the three-fold nature of God: God the Father, God the Son, and God the Holy Ghost. The longest season of the Christian year, it lasts through the summer until Advent.

The first part of the year deals with Jesus himself, His birth, His life, the Crucifixion, the Resurrection, His Ascension, and the return of the Holy Spirit. Now, in this second part, the essence of God's relationship to the individual and to the world is primary, and the Church becomes the medium through which God must work for the salvation of all men.

White is appropriate for the first Sunday of Trinity, and through the next one. Following the second Sunday in Trinity, green is the liturgical color. Plate 54 shows three all-white designs using large forms which stand out best in the dark church. Another all-white Trinity

Plate 54

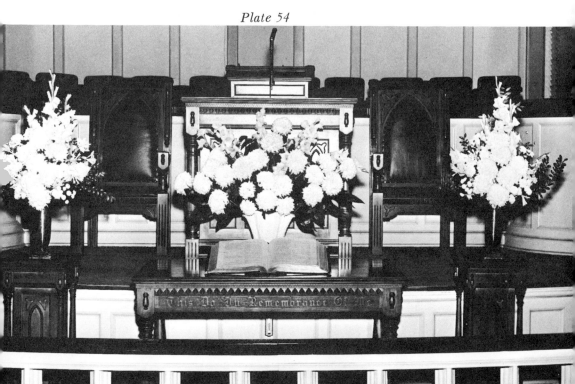

Plate 55

design in an equilateral triangle appropriate to the Three-in-One symbolism is shown in Plate 55. White chrysanthemums, daisies, gladioli and roses are the materials.

Mass arrangements of summer flowers fill the church during the Trinity season. Plate 56 shows a design made by Marguerite Bozarth for the chapel at Sandpoint Community Methodist Church in Seattle, Washington.

Garden flowers (variegated pink and white carnations, three shades of pink roses, and pale lavender blossoms of hosta) are shown on a walnut altar. The compote and the candlesticks are of brass; the candles are ivory. Note that the flower arrangement is higher than the candles, and there is no reason why this should not be done. However, it is usual practice to give an altar cross the eminent position—it should be higher than either the candles or the flower arrangements placed on the altar.

Trinity Symbols

A triangle of three interlocking circles symbolic of the Trinity is used on the paraments on Trinity Sunday. Other symbols are the fleur-de-lis, flower arrangements in a triangle shape (in the church, equilateral ones best express the meaning of the season), the trillium lily, and any material with three distinctly equal parts.

Plate 56

Plate 57

Trinity in the Home

Triangular arrangements for the home or garden club continue to be appropriate. Plate 57 features scrub oak, yellow roses and dahlias in a green glass container which contrasted with the shaggy texture of the plant material.

A more formal summer arrangement is shown in Plate 58. Marguerite Bozarth features summer flowers, and includes the trillium lily which, with its three leaves capped by a solitary flower, symbolizes this season.

As summer wanes, autumn flowers in their bright, warm, advancing hues appear in the garden. Plate 59 shows red-orange canna foliage, Mexican sunflower, (tithonia) orange-yellow daisies, and contrasted blue asters and hydrangea, with tawny grapes on the orange base.

Plate 58   Plate 59

IV

Flowers for Other Christian Occasions

1. THE SACRAMENT OF BAPTISM

By one spirit we are all baptised into one body. I Corinthians 12:13

This sacrament, representing the grace which removes the taint of previous sin from the soul, is essential for salvation in churches believing in original sin. The mode or rite of administering Baptism varies according to the doctrines of each church. The three different ways of applying the water are *infusion*—pouring on the head; *aspersion*—sprinkling; and *immersion*. Since the baptism of infants is encouraged, the name *christening* (making Christian) is used as a synonym for Baptism. Of ancient origin is the use of the 8-pointed star to symbolize the baptism. From this origin has come the custom of designing the baptismal font with eight sides.

Plate 60 shows a mass triangle designed for use during the baptismal or christening service. It would do equally well in the home or church. Tuberoses form the outline with white dahlias, roses, ligustrum and pittosporum. All-white designs are appropriate in all Christian seasons —although the paraments or hangings are designated according to liturgy—since white blends with all colors and as a symbol of purity is always correct. However, many flower arrangers seem to forget that color is as much a gift as the flowers themselves, and the glory of color should not be overlooked in the right time and place.

Plate 60

2. THE SACRAMENT OF COMMUNION

What communion hath light with darkness. 2 Corinthians 6:14

Communion is the celebration of the Lord's Supper as a separate service. Some churches serve communion every week, some every second week, others every two months, and one serves communion every three months.

In the Episcopal church, before the communicant goes to the altar rail he recites the Nicean Creed, which tells how Christ suffered and died. Because white is a symbol of purity, white flowers are most frequently used for communion observances. Plate 61 shows a lovely church setting for a Communion Sunday. Mrs. D. C. Huskey of Fort Pierce, Florida, arrangement an assortment of white chrysanthe-

Plate 61

mums both small and large, in a pair of brass vases with an open bible placed between them. A window above the altar set in a contemporary brick wall sheds a rose glow on the cross seen against dark red velvet.

Holy Communion or the Lord's Supper is a sacrament ordained by Christ, its symbols being bread and wine, consecrated elements which are consumed by the congregants. Thus, wheat and grapes are full of spiritual implications for the Christian.

Plate 62 shows an arrangement for communion using wheat and grapes. World-wide Communion Day is October 1.

3. WORLD DAY OF PRAYER

The right hands of fellowship. Galatians 11:9

World Day of Prayer, now eighty years old, is observed on the first Friday of Lent in 125 countries on six continents around the globe. It is world-wide in character because the same order of service translated into many different languages is used in all parts of the world.

Plate 62

The design in Plate 63 features Albrecht Dürer's sculpture "Praying Hands," often used in ecclesiastical arrangements. They are shown with roses and an antique mahogany Bishop's chair in an arrangement by Mrs. Raymond P. Wismer.

4. CHURCH WEDDINGS

The Christian wedding, and especially a church wedding, is a moving affirmation of faith and belief in the future. Flowers help to set the stage for the drama of this high point in life, and to enrich its meaning with their beautiful symbolism. The purity of the bride, the tenderness of the groom, the freshness and gaiety of the occasion are marked with the flowers which transform the church or chapel. And when the wedding is at home, whether indoors or out in the garden, under a canopy or on a city terrace, then flowers bring to the more prosaic settings the aura of the higher meaning of the church.

There are traditional places in a church for flowers for a wedding, and perhaps this is because they best enrich the architecture of the church. As in other ceremonies, the main attention is focused on the altar, and the sanctuary, where the ceremony will occur.

The pathway down the center of the church should lead, visually, to this center of attention. Thus, the decorations on the pews should not be over-elaborate, or have bouquets that are too large, as they may interfere with the view or the passage of the wedding procession.

In Plate 64 we see an example of a wedding decoration that is fairly restrained although lovely and appropriate. The topiary trees are constructed with chicken wire, and filled with sphagnum moss and Oasis. White roses, chrysanthemums, and tuberoses are used for the trees.

The Trinity Church of Deland, Florida, is seen in Plate 65 with a much more elaborate floral display—with the pew ends to the altar and the rails festooned. Tree ferns furnish a pleasing background for the arrangement in the choir loft and the altar. The candelabra on either side are used for balance. The plant materials are white gladiolus, mums, roses, and ferns. The tree ferns (or standards) are usually constructed on styrofoam blocks, wired to a sturdy holder. The Oregon flat fern is preferred.

Plate 63

Plate 64

Plate 65

Pews are often decorated for the church wedding, Plate 66 features white gladioli, stock, chrysanthemums, candles and ribbons.

Basic Color Themes

White and rare flowers are used traditionally with white and more formal weddings. With the ivory tone, frequently used in the bride's gown, pale yellow flowers harmonize in a delicate way. Less formal pastel gowns, the slightly orchid, ice blue, pink, all call for delicately shaded flowers that enhance the gown color.

But while the basic color theme may vary from the white of roses, phalaenopsis, cattleya orchids and stephanotis to the vivid reds of carnations and roses, there is contrast and harmony to be found in the bridesmaids' bouquets, the corsages, boutonnieres and the arrangements for the bridal party and bridal table.

Plate 66

The seasonal aspect of decorating for a wedding is of great importance. A spring wedding lends itself to flowers that may range from the tender simplicity of the branches of dogwood that lined a dado above the bench where the bride and groom sat holding hands at a Quaker wedding, to the triangle of cut hyacinth, white tulip and dogwood that mounted to the cross at a formal wedding at St. James, fashionable Episcopal Church on Fifth Avenue in New York.

Dogwood is a particularly favorable flower for spring weddings, with the pink or white varieties used. The blossoms give an effect of airiness and spring, and seem to harmonize with the mood of the ceremony. Masses of other delicate spring blossoms may be used, such as peach and apple branches, forsythia, crabapple, plum or wild cherry. Potted tulips (in pink or white) and lilacs in great bunches also make spring weddings memorable.

A summer bride is also fortunate, with spirea, peonies and snowballs for altar bouquets and gladioli for tall vases, as well as spikes of delphinium and clouds of babies'-breath.

The fall wedding has a more dramatic quality with the rich tones of chrysanthemums, asters, daisies, marigolds and bold zinnias.

Winter weddings have the sparkle of the holidays—and can share in the seasonal decorations of the church. Bouquets and corsages have small Christmas tree balls and Christmas trees lighted by tiny candles massed on the altar to provide an unforgettable background.

Corsages and Bouquets

The flowers that the bride and the other members of the wedding carry are determined by fairly rigid protocol and depend on the degree of formality of the ceremony, the season, the attire worn by the bride, the mothers, bridesmaids, and attendants, and of course by the preferences of the bride.

The Reception

Celebrating a wedding with feasting and fun is a custom that goes back to and beyond Biblical times, and dependence upon flowers to provide the wedding atmosphere is also a long established tradition.

In addition to the bouquets for bride and bridesmaid, flowers belong on the bridal table, the wedding cake table, the buffet, the guest tables, if the guests are to be seated, and the punch table. If the wedding reception is informal, one dining table may do the work of all of these, but arrangements provide the note of festivity and beauty to the occasion. A cupid compote is seen in Plate 67, and this rhythmic design could be used in the reception hall or some place where a large design is needed. Its main line is established with ivy, symbol of fidelity in marriage. The flowers could be any garden or florist ones including daylilies, dahlias, roses, gladioli, daisies, and many others.

Wedding Anniversaries

Wedding anniversaries are often celebrated with services in the church and receptions at home. Plate 68 shows an arrangement for a silver aniversary. Fresh tuberoses are a symbol of today, silvered driftwood is a link with yesterday, and the modern abstract container is a tie to tomorrow.

Plate 67

Plate 68

Fresh tuberoses repeat the flowers used in the wedding bouquet a quarter of a century ago, the abstract container shows the bride is a modern flower arranger and the silver driftwood is the link which relates each to the other. Another silver anniversary design, Plate 69, shows aspidistra leaves sprayed with silver tinsel, gladioli, chrysanthemums, delphiniums, and grapes, symbol of joy and revelry.

Two designs planned for a fiftieth wedding are shown. Plate 70 is designed around the antique figurine of a woman ringing a wedding bell. Orchids and grapes are used with gilded weathered wood and a gilded frame. Plate 71 shows a gold stand and gilded manzanita wood with pink carnations for first love and red roses for deep love at the center of interest.

Plate 69   *Plate 70 opposite*

Plate 71

V

Secular Days Observed in the Church and Home

Many secular holidays have roots deep in religious observances. The ancient Greeks dedicated their yearly spring festival to Rhea, mythical mother of gods and goddesses. The early Christians honored all mothers during the month of May which, in fact, is named after Mary, the mother of Christ. In England on "mothering Sunday," which usually fell on the fourth Sunday of Lent, it was the custom to allow servants a free day for visits to their mothers and families.

1. MOTHER'S AND FATHER'S DAYS

Mother's Day, observed the second Sunday in May (and in schools the preceding Friday), was originated by Anna M. Jarvis to honor all American mothers, and she named the carnation as the official flower. Thus, the tradition of giving flowers to mothers began in 1914 and has continued through the years.

For Father's Day (which falls on the third Sunday in June) the featured flower is the rose. However, it is quite usual for floral designers to make mixed bouquets for either day.

Mother's Day

Plate 72 shows 2 pair of vases at the altar using the symbolic carnation enhanced by a tuberose and pittosporum. Here, we mention again that details are more vital in church arrangements than in any other. Bold large flowers, scintillating colors, and a well-designed pattern are essential. One should remember that the audience must look at them or toward them for one hour. They should appeal to visual perception and inner emotions.

A simple but charming tribute to mother, Plate 73, is arranged for the altar by Marguerite Bozarth. A ceramic vase and brass candlesticks with white candles are shown with vivid red carnations, pale pink and white roses, and yellow irises.

Arrangements to take to Mother or to use in one's own home feature the best from the newly blooming garden. They bespeak the grace and tenderness of motherhood, ranging from the highly devout to the sentimental and old-fashioned in spirit.

What could be more fitting for Mother's day in the church social hall or at home than a design with a figurine accessory such as the one shown in Plate 74? Geraniums and roses are the flowers. Another arrangement featuring a figurine, this time as a container, is shown in Plate 75. It holds white roses and tuberoses and is placed on a Florentine gold table.

Plate 72

Plate 73

Plate 74

Plate 75

Father's Day

Father's Day is celebrated more and more in the home and the church. Honoring the man of the house with a flower arrangement may seem inappropriate, since one usually associates Mother, rather than Father, with floral design. But millions of men are dedicated spare-time horticulturists, and an arrangement featuring blossoms he has grown would be a most telling compliment. One design by a man—and there are many men who arrange flowers as a hobby—is shown in Plate 76. The work of Mr. John C. Dowling, Jr. of Gaffney, South Carolina, it combines roses, a sturdy palm spathe, and a rugged driftwood sculpture. Since the rose is the official flower for Father's Day, it is always a good selection.

Another version of flowers for Father, Plate 77, shows red roses given masculine support by the rough texture of the blue-green yew foliage. Sea-grape leaves in the off-white container set off the flowers from the container.

Plate 76   *Plate 77*

Of course, there is a large group of gardeners who refuse to allow blossoms to be cut from their prize bushes, no matter in whose honor the cutting is done. For such fathers, a potted plant in a handsome planter will be a more tactful gift, especially if you tuck a rose into his lapel to further signify your love.

The strongly architectural design in Plate 78 honors father with deep pink to red roses, and ferns. The container subtly reminds Father that you think he is as steady and dependable as St. Peter.

Plate 78

2. PATRIOTIC DAYS

I will hear what God the Lord will speak: for he will speak
peace unto his people, and to his saints; but let them not
turn again to folly. Psalm 85:8

Along with the rest of the nation, the church celebrates special days
of patriotism and dedication such as July Fourth and Memorial Day.
These are days that call for vibrant testimonials, with stirring words
from the pulpit and with a riot of available flowers and foliage (since
flowers are increasingly recognized as speaking the language of peace
and freedom).

John Adams' letter to his wife, following the adoption of Inde-
pendence Day, the Fourth of July in 1776 is pertinent:

I am apt to believe that this day will be celebrated by succeeding generations
as the great anniversary festival. It ought to be commemorated as the day of
deliverance, by solemn acts of devotion to Almighty God. It ought to be solemn-
ized with pomp and parade, with shows, games, sports, guns, bells, bonfires and
illumination from one end of the Continent to the other, from this time forward
forevermore.

For a summer altar, the informal arrangement shown in Plate 57
would be charming. It features crepe-myrtle, wild roses, lilies, and
cleomes.

In Plate 79, a gold eagle high above the fruits and flowers leads
one to think of freedom to work and freedom to enjoy the fruit of
one's labor. The eagle, our most commonly used symbol of freedom
and national symbol, is a link with the church since St. Jerome, who
called the eagle the symbol of Ascension and of prayer, and Dante
who called it the "bird of God"—an allusion to its higher powers.

Labor Day

And the Lord God took the man, and put him into the
Garden of Eden to dress it and keep it. Genesis 2:15

Another secular holiday which is marked in our churches is Labor
Day, celebrated on the first Monday in September. The churches
usually have special programs the Sunday preceding Labor Day. It is
interesting to know something about the origins of this holiday.

Labor Day began 83 years ago, when Peter J. McGuire, president of the United Brotherhood of Carpenters and Joiners of America and an active leader in the Knights of Labor, suggested the date because it fell midway between July Fourth and Thanksgiving. And, in those days of penny wages and long hours, labor truly needed a breather.

New York's Central Labor Union turned out that first Monday of September, 1882, for its Labor Day parade, and Oregon in 1887 declared the first state holiday in honor of labor. By 1894, thirty states had taken a similar action. Congress passed a bill recognizing Labor Day as a national holiday the same year.

In the Christian ethic, man is put on earth to labor, and this in the Bible is synonymous with tending one's garden.

And in the Proverbs it is written:

Plate 79

I went by the field of the slothful, and by the vineyard of the man void of understanding: and lo, it was all grown over with thorns, and nettles had covered the face thereof, and the stone wall thereof was broken down. Then I saw and considered it well. I looked upon it and received instructions. PROVERBS 24:30-32

Flowers and fruits of work, therefore, are fitting symbols for this day.

Plate 80 shows snapdragons, gladioli, chrysanthemums and peppers in a triangular harmony. An interpretative design, its inspiration was "For we are labourers together with God." (Corinthians 3:9).

The walnut wood compote and base set the tone for the design in Plate 81. Branches of rosemary, sign of remembrance, are used with seasonal plant material in yellow to deep orange to brown.

Thanksgiving—Abundance in the Christian Spirit

When thou has eaten and art full then thou shalt bless the
Lord thy God for the good land which He hath given thee.
Deuteronomy 8:10

Harvest festivals are an ancient ceremony still observed in England and in other countries, where crosses fashioned of corn, and giant sheaves of wheat, are bought into the church to celebrate the gathering of the crop.

In America, the last Thursday in November is made a legal holiday by an annual proclamation of the President and the state governors. A legacy of the Pilgrims, perhaps the most distinctly American holiday we have, it was first proclaimed by Governor Bradford of Plymouth, who announced a day of Thanksgiving for the abundant harvests of "Plymouth Colony." He sent out hunters who returned with turkeys, thus establishing the custom of having a turkey on this special day.

Wheat and pumpkins may be arranged around the cross with gourds at the rear table in the center, and fall flowers in the altar vases and urns. Flowers in vivid colors seem particularly appropriate. The designs in the altar vases shown in Plate 82, while restrained, are expressive of Thanksgiving plenty. Made on a styrofoam base, which is shaped into a vertical form with a three-inch cut to fit into the container, each design includes fruits pinned on with florist pins. The magnolia leaves are yellow, brown and gold, touched by autumn magic. Rhododendron leaves could be substituted, as well as innumerable others, glycerinized or fresh. (See Chapter VI, Section 4, for a list of other foliages.)

Plate 80

Plate 81

Plate 82

The arrangement shown in Plate 83 uses fresh cut firethorn (pyracantha) berries in an asymmetrical line. Garden flowers make the center of interest—yellow, yellow-orange, and orange-red—a striking analagous color harmony for the church in Autumn.

Thanksgiving is also a time of home worship when, in a spirit of appreciation and devotion, the family gathers around the table, truly a festive board, heaped as it is with the best from Mother's kitchen. The dining room, and the Thanksgiving table particularly, echo this tribute:

O give thanks unto the Lord; for he is good; for His mercy endureth forever. I Chronicles 16:34

Containers for this season are reminiscent of the first Thanksgivings— the brass pottery of Colonial times, and the simplicity of early harvests. Thus, a centerpiece of a small wooden tub might be filled with orange chrysanthemums, and might hold a single white candle. Pewter tankards, bright provincial ware, daisies, geraniums, stoneware crocks, all suggest the earthiness and humble beginnings of Thanksgiving.

The horn of plenty is so associated with Thanksgiving that to have a chapter on this theme without it would be unthinkable. In Plate 84 we have included a wicker horn of plenty filled and running over with the beautiful fruits, vegetables, flowers and foliage of our great land.

An unusual table decoration for Thanksgiving is shown in Plate 85.

Autumn colors and fruits are combined effectively in an asymmetrical design. This line is formed by glycerinized variegated aspidistra leaves with dried magnolia foliage on the right. Dried dock, fresh cut amber chrysanthemums, and orange-red grapes finish the arrangement.

Another arrangement for this season is shown in Plate 86—fall flowers and vegetables and a pair of game birds recall the Pilgrim hunters who provided the good food for the first Thanksgiving.

Finally, a simple yet bold little arrangement in a sturdy earthenware pitcher speaks of autumn (Plate 87). A gray-green earthenware pitcher holds castor bean seed pods and foliage (the Spanish call it palm of Christ, and it may be the gourd referred to in the Bible). The gray on the back of the leaf is a good hue for the light values on the smooth pitcher. The dark green plant material harmonizes with the upper part of the container, and the seed pods give excellent contrast in color and texture.

Plate 83

Plate 84

Plate 85

Plate 86

Plate 87

VI

The Church, the Club, and You

1. POINTERS FOR THE ALTAR GUILD

The Altar Guild, organized by the minister and working under his direction, performs a form of Christian service which lay members are usually happy to participate in. Most Altar Guilds meet once a month. Typically, a short devotional period precedes the assignment of specific duties to the committees of each department.

The general chairman of the Altar Guild heads from one to five committees, depending on the size of the church and the number of members it serves. The most important committee is the Steward's Committee for the communion service. It prepares the elements (bread and wine), placing them on the Altar with the cups to serve the Holy Communion to individuals who are participating. After the service of this Sacrament is finished, the stewards remove all the elements and wash and store the vessels.

The Flower Committee has the responsibility of arranging flowers for Sundays and all occasions. If the florist does the arranging, the flower chairman makes certain that the color and designs are appropriate; this is most important if the Church is a liturgical one. This committee also places and removes the flowers from the altar. Usually these are sent to the sick at home or in the hospital.

Still another important committee, headed by a chairman, must be responsible for caring for the linen, polishing the candlesticks and vases, and seeing to it that the collection plates are available when needed. The chairman and wedding committee function through the guild, explaining to the florist what he can do in the way of decorations on the church property. (Vases must be waterproof; baskets may not be placed on the rug without proper protection, etc.) One member of the committee, usually the chairman, should be on hand during the preparation. As a timesaver, mimeographed instructions may be prepared and distributed to the florist and others concerned with the floral decorations. Whether the church is large or small, the guild should have a memorial committee. This special group secures flowers for each Sunday of the year from individuals who wish to remember some loved one. The flowers are used during worship service, and then removed to the cemetery, or given to the sick by the flower committee.

Since symbolism becomes vivid only when it is familiar, I urge you to lose no opportunity to explain the tradition behind your usage of specific flowers and objects.

An interesting article written by Kate Clapp about new trends in altar guild practice appeared recently in The Akron (Ohio) *Beacon Journal:*

Years ago, flowers for the church were of secondary consideration. At Easter, Christmastime, and for several memorial occasions during the year there were potted plants on the altar or big stiff baskets of flowers from the florist. This was particularly true of small churches or those in suburban areas where seemingly little consideration was given to the artistic value of the flowers or their effectiveness in keeping with the décor of the church itself. I remember Children's day, long ago, when everyone brought vases of a heterogeneous mixture of half wilted June blossoms picked at the last minute 'so they would be fresh.' The result was pathetic.

But no more! In most churches today there is an altar guild made up of dedicated flower arrangers who take their duties seriously, planning for the effectiveness of the flowers to be viewed from the front to the back of the sanctuary. Guild members consider the immediate background color at the reredos, the woodwork, walls, carpeting, and lighting, and use floral colors that enhance the beauty of the church and add to the feeling of worship. The arrangements shown are for Sunday morning services at the Community Church at Bath . . . the altar is white with rich red wall drapery against which the altar and pulpit have a dramatic effect.

The Church flower arrangement committee has 15 members . . . each member has a turn in fixing altar flowers for the Sunday services. Flowers are fixed and placed Saturday afternoon for the Sunday services.

Two summer arrangements made for effective display against the dark red curtains in the Community Church at Bath, Ohio, are shown. Plate 88 by Mrs. John A. MacKay and Mrs. Charles Reeder features pale yellow lemon lilies and feverfew. Plate 89 by Mrs. Ralph Anderson uses the popular new Powderpuff hollyhock in shades of red and soft deep rose, with white chrysanthemums to define them from the curtain, and euonymus leaves.

Plate 89

Plate 88

2. COLORS, LIGHTING, AND PLACEMENT

Some churches are so gorgeously ornamented and filled with objects that the arrangements, eye-filling, lovely and inspiring though they may be, are only one in a series of beautiful things seen by the worshipper. The arrangements in such a site must be bold and strong, with colors grouped in good-sized areas, rather than scattered spottily throughout. Mass arrangements in a clearly defined form—vertical, triangular, oval or crescent generally carry best across the church, and are best able to hold their own with other decorations. However, in a small church against a plain background, massed line designs or even line designs may be quite satisfactory.

Lighting may be a problem. Often a beautiful mass arrangement fails to carry because the lighting is inadequate. New churches have accent lights built in for flower arrangement, and the table holding the flowers or the flower stand can be picked out by a spot in exciting and masterful ways, just as the lighting designer for the theatre picks out his spots of color.

In the conventional Gothic church, the eastern or altar end may be in a critical place. If there is a window, the wall below it is left in shadow. In such a site, luminous yellows, bright orange, and clear tones of red, green, and blue are effective.

In many New England and Southern churches, however, the opposite condition prevails, and bright sunlight floods the church, washing out the arrangements. Here is the place where dark blues, and greens can be effective. White is excellent, of course, against any dark background. The densely patterned foliages shown in the arrangements in Plates 90 and 91 would be clearly visible in brightly lighted churches but would be lost against busy, dark, or poorly lighted areas. Plate 90 uses Norfolk Island pine, sansevieria, roses, hibiscus, and the bloom of artichokes. Plate 90 has an outline of Japanese yew with dahlias at the center of interest.

Texture is an important aspect of this subject, and colors may appear quite different if their surfaces vary. Smooth, glossy surfaces reflect more light; they are ethereal and depict brightness and femininity. Rough glossy finishes are strong and lively, but less luminous than smooth, glossy finishes. Rough matte textures are masculine, deliberate, important; while smooth matte surfaces are neutral, stable, faces are neutral, stable, and tranquil. In Plate 92, the liveliness of the textured pine and the masculinity of the rough sumac seed pods are good foils for glossy day lilies and the smooth, light-reflecting container.

Plate 90 top left

Plate 91 top right

Plate 92 opposite

If the church is large, flowers should be tall enough to be seen at eye level from the rear. Test visibility from one of the seats at the back.

Be sure that the flowers are placed so they do not interfere with the service.

Finally, good taste dictates that the altar cross should always stand higher than the flowers.

3. THE MECHANICS AND TOOLS OF ARRANGEMENT

All the meaning, the spirit, the beauty of materials, the color and careful placement, will come to nothing if the materials are not fresh and the arrangement is not sturdy and well balanced. To have an arrangement topple over during service is an Altar Guild nightmare, and it is always sad when expensive materials and time-consuming designs arrive at the church fading and drooping.

Vases and containers may be packed with sand or stones to weight them down. Elaborate designs that require supports should be firmly welded or nailed. Look for objects that will stand firmly on their bases. Avoid branches that get in the way of ushers or others taking part in the service (such as the crucifer or taperers).

Oasis, Vermiculite, crushed chicken wire, needle-point holder, (cup type), Spanish moss and ferns are all especially appropriate for the tall container. Vermiculite may be purchased at the builder's supply, Oasis at the florist.

Oasis is perhaps the best, easiest, and cleanest to use. It can be prepared by soaking it in water for five minutes and wrapped in foil, it is ready for use. The irises and jonquils in Plate 93 are kept fresh in Oasis wrapped in foil and inserted into openings in the wood. (Incidentally, children are fascinated by mobile compositions; this one includes two doves.) Oasis is also useful when fresh and dried materials are combined, for it provides enough water to sustain the former and not enough to induce rot in the latter. Plate 94 combines dried dock, aspidistra leaves, and magnolia foliage with fresh flowers.

Vermiculite, on the other hand, must be pressed into the container, watered and pressed some more until it is packed enough to hold plant material securely. An ice pick, or pencil, should be used to make the hole for placement of fragile flowers. It is excellent in transparent containers because of its neutral color. In Plate 95 it provides the mechanics for an S-line arrangement in glass.

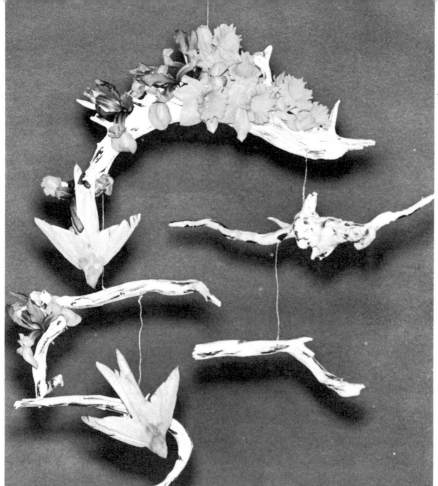

Plate 93

Plate 95

Plate 94

The pin-cup needle point holder is ideal to place on top of a container which has a small opening. It can be secured by masking tape placed in front and behind. The front can be covered by placing plant material over the lip of the container, as in Plate 96. Another use for the pin-cup holder is shown in Plate 97. The bottom of the pin-cup is covered with a ring of floral clay, which is then pressed firmly down against the inside of the container. Both holder and container must be clean and dry or the clay won't hold. Water in the pin-cup keeps the gladioli and daisies fresh.

Sometimes, however, even this holder is too small for the amount of plant material you wish to use. In that case, make a funnel of Oasis, soak it in water, wrap it in foil, and stick the narrow end into the container, using the wide end to hold the flowers and foliage. In Plate 98, the Oasis was pinned to wire mesh, and set in an abstract container to hold white John F. Kennedy roses. The design was made for World Day of Prayer.

Wire in many different sizes is needed for wiring leaves, roses and flowers with weak stems. Foliage, such as aspidistra, can be wired with Scotch tape, thus making it usable in a variety of ways. Modeling clay is a useful item to have on hand. Even a stapler can help the flower arranger. Plate 99 shows loops of palmetto palm which have been stapled in desired shapes and arranged with red anthuriums and white tuberoses.

"Twistems," wire and other tying material, such as, thread or string are useful in holding together small stems. Plumbers' lead is excellent to hold plant material in place at the lip of the container especially if it is glass.

Small and large pruning shears, a kitchen knife, scissors and clippers will be needed for the cutting of the plant material. Water picks, floral picks, (several different lengths) and cocktail picks are important items in the arrangers basket. Styrofoam can be used as a base, or it can be cut into small pieces and used as wedges.

Plate 96   *top left*

Plate 97   *top right*

Plate 98   *left*

Plate 99

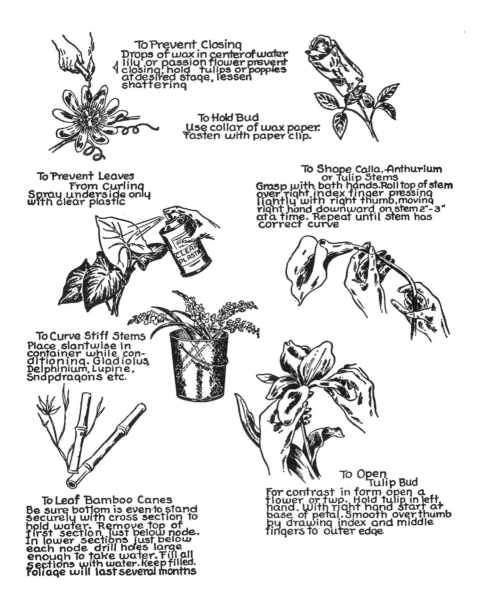

To Prevent Closing
Drops of wax in center of water lily or passion flower prevent closing; hold tulips or poppies at desired stage, lessen shattering

To Hold Bud
Use collar of wax paper. Fasten with paper clip.

To Prevent Leaves From Curling
Spray underside only with clear plastic

To Shape Calla, Anthurium or Tulip Stems
Grasp with both hands. Roll top of stem over right index finger pressing lightly with right thumb, moving right hand downward on stem 2"-3" at a time. Repeat until stem has correct curve

To Curve Stiff Stems
Place slantwise in container while conditioning. Gladiolus, Delphinium, Lupine, Snapdragons etc.

To Leaf Bamboo Canes
Be sure bottom is even to stand securely with cross section to hold water. Remove top of first section just below node. In lower sections just below each node drill holes large enough to take water. Fill all sections with water. Keep filled. Foliage will last several months

To Open Tulip Bud
For contrast in form open a flower or two. Hold tulip in left hand. With right hand start at base of petal. Smooth over thumb by drawing index and middle fingers to outer edge

Drawings by Charlotte E. Bowden and Charles A. Mahoney from *Gardening, Forcing, Conditioning and Drying for Flower Arrangements,* by Arno and Irene Nehrling, reprinted courtesy of the publishers, Hearthside Press, Inc., New York.

CUTTING and CONDITIONING for ARRANGEMENTS

Enjoy Rhododendron blossoms indoors. Cut branches from crowded places that need thinning. Where branches will not be missed. From long shoots that need shortening. Just above a node for good branching.

Use boxwood or yew clippings decoratively at Christmas time Cut short ends here and there around the entire plant. Good way to keep plant the desired size

Carry pail of warm water to garden. Cut flowers with sharp knife (NOT SCISSORS) Use diagonal cut. Remove unnecessary leaves. Place stems in warm water at once. Leave in pail overnight in cool place

Cut berried spray of Pyracantha. Choose one that wont be missed. Cut above a node. Remove thorns any leaves that hide colorful fruit.

Revive prematurely wilted flowers. Recut stem ends. Place in warm to hot water (80° to 100° F) Recondition overnight.

80°-100° WATER

To condition evergreen branches
Wash in warm soapy water. Rinse in cold water. Remove defective leaves, thin if too full. Split stem ends 2"-3" Place in warm water, condition overnight or longer. Use one tablespoon of glycerin to each quart of water.

ONE TABLESPOON   ONE QT.   TO EACH QUART

To condition Ivies
Cut just above a node for good branching Submerge mature foliage in cold water for 4 hours. Young tender foliage 1 hour. Insert stems in water filled orchid tubes for vegetable and fruit arrangements

Scotch Broom.
Cut branches desired length clean in cold water split woody stems. Tie branches bent to curves wanted. Submerge in cold water several hours Dry, then untie.

Spray berried or needled branches with a clear plastic to decrease the shriveling and falling of berries or needles.

How To Force Flowering Branches

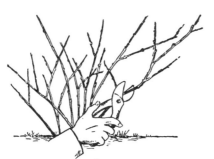

Cut branches with sharp tool on a mild day

Soak branches in bath tub for 24 hours

Crush stems with hammer to aid water intake

Place branches deep in water until buds break

Place in sunny window for flowering

4. USEFUL PLANT MATERIAL

White flowers: Agapanthus, amaryllis, anemone, azalea, buddleia,
camellia, carnation, chrysanthemum, cyclamen, daffodil, dahlia,
delphinium, dianthus, dogwood, gardenia, gladiolus, gypsophila,
helleborus, hibiscus, hydrangea, hyssop, (sweet marjoram), lilac,
lily (Easter, Madonna), lily of the valley, magnolia, narcissus,
peony, petunia, phlox, pieris, rose, rose of sharon, shasta daisy,
snapdragon, spirea, stock, trillium, tuberose, tulip, zinnia, and
many others.

Pink flowers: amaryllis, anemone, aster, azalea, carnation, chrysanthemum, cleome, coleus, columbine, cosmos, coxcomb, dahlia, day
lily, dianthus, geranium, gladiolus, gourds, hyacinth, hyssop, oriental poppy, peony, phlox, ranunculus, rose, rose of sharon, snapdragon, tulip, zinnia.

Blue and violet flowers: Aconitum, agapanthus, ageratum, anchusa,
aster, balloon flower, buddleia, canterbury bells, chrysanthemums,
clematis, clover, cobaea, columbine, cornflowers, coxcomb, dahlia,
delphinium, dianthus, gladiolus, helleborus orientalis, hosta, hyacinth, hydrangea, hyssop, larkspur, lilac, lobelia, pansies, petunia,
rhododendron, salvia, scabiosa, stock, sweet pea, thistle, tulip,
violets, weigela, wisteria.

Yellow to orange flowers: butterfly weed, calla lily, chrysanthemum,
columbine, coreopsis, coxcomb, dahlia, day lily, forsythia, gladiolus, gourds, grittonia, hibiscus, iris, lily (auratum), marigold, narcissus, pansies, pyracantha berry, rose, snapdragon, tulip.

Red flowers: anemone, California poppy, celosia, chrysanthemums,
cleome, coleus, coreopsis, cosmos, dahlia, dianthus, gaillardia,
hollyhock, lobelia, marigold, Mexican fire plant, rhododendron,
salvia, snapdragons, strawflower, tritonia, tulips, zinnia.

Long-lasting foliage (those marked with an asterisk dry well): andro-
meda, aspidistra, *beech, canna, castor-oil plant, cedar branches,
coleus, croton, dieffenbachia, dracaena, *eleagnus, *eucalyptus,
euonymus, evergreens, *ferns, *grape, *grasses, holly, hosta,
huckleberry, ivy, laurel, leucothe, *magnolia, mahonia,oak, palm,
pandanus, peach branches, pine, pittosporum, podocarpus, rhododendron, sansevieria, white poplar, etc.

Glycerine will preserve foliage of many plants such as barberry, beech, dogwood, eleagnus, ivy, laurel, magnolia, plum, rhododendron, viburnum, etc. The procedure: Clean the foliage, cut the end of the bark for an inch or two (to increase absorption) and place in a jar holding one part glycerine to two parts water. After two or more weeks, leaves will absorb solution.

Don't overlook such materials as wild ferns and grasses, wheat, and shrubs. Flowering shrubs and trees, such as quince, white and pink dogwood, Scotch broom, forsythia, leucothoe, magnolia, honeysuckle, rhododendron, Japanese maple, birch, pear and cherry blossoms can be cut in winter and early spring. Brought indoors and set in a pail of water, they will bloom early. Place in a sunny window to hasten the flowering process.

Evergreen branches supply beautiful foliage the year round.

5. SUGGESTED FLOWER SHOW THEMES

Flower show committees should write their schedules keeping in mind the needs of their own community. Availability of plants, the site and seasons for the show, and the tastes and abilities of the arranger-exhibitors should be considered.

There is no reason to exclude modern floral art from the church or the flower show. The manzanita branch in Plate 100 has been reversed

Plate 100

in line with the best modern-abstract practice yet the design fits the Bible quotation for which it was planned—"Behold the day, behold, it is come: the morning is gone forth; the rod hath blossomed, pride hath budded." Ezekiel 9:10.

Themes and classes can be developed around the subjects covered in Chapter 2 on symbolism—Bible plant materials, colors, fauna, crosses, etc. Or they can be developed around just one symbol. For example, the theme could be Stars in the Bible. There are references to stars to Genesis 1:16; Job 38:7, Daniel 12:3, 1 Corinthians 15:4; 22:16, and Revelations 8:10; 9:7, among others. Imagination should be used by the committee to achieve variety. For the class ". . . and I saw a star fall from heaven to earth." inspired by Revelation 9:1, for example, the requirement could be a mobile using stars, (Plate 101), a mobile best reflecting a falling star. For the quotation from Genesis, the class could require a black and white arrangement featuring a star, to reflect the "night and day" aspect of the quotation.

The schedules could give appropriate symbols, specify the use of liturgical colors, give themes based on the eight events of the Christian year, provide classes featuring representational animal figurines for juniors, and in other ways inspire exhibitors to do meaningful work. Ecumenical placement flower shows held at different churches in town would be an exciting and inspirational event for the whole community.

Neatly and uniformly printed cards quoting the Bible passage should be displayed as a means of educating the public.

6. PROGRAMS FOR JUNIORS

Now let's think about programs and exhibitions for children. It is so easy to teach them the Bible—building their enthusiasm, creating wholehearted cooperation—by relating the gospel to objects they love: flowers, sea shells, (Plate 102) insects, animals (Plate 103) nature in general. Why not plan a series of programs, selecting appropriate quotations about the fauna of the Bible? The quotations could be mimeographed, and children could be encouraged to create their own animals from papier mache, drawing them free-hand, or cutting them out of magazines, and mounting them on cardboard. The use of flowers, driftwood, pine cones, and other plant materials should be encouraged to make the scene either pictorial or interpretative of the Biblical quotation which inspired it.

Plate 101

Plate 102

Plate 103

7. INSPIRATION FROM THE BIBLE

CLASS I   *"Awake, O North wind; and come Thou upon my Garden."*
           Solomon 4:16

           A design showing motion, using fresh flowers and foliage.

CLASS II   *"For lo the winter is past the rain is over and gone."* Solomon
           2:11

           A design using driftwood and budding branches. Minimum
           amount of spring flowers permitted.

CLASS III *"Evening and morning and noon will I pray."* Psalms 55:17

           A design of all fresh plant material, using an accessory
           indicative of prayer. Accessory may be featured.

CLASS IV   *"They took branches of palm trees and went forth to meet
           him."* John 12:13

           A design with palm material dominant, sago permitted.
           Minimum amount of other fresh foliage permitted.

CLASS V   *"And Jonah was in the belly of the fish."* Jonah 1:17

           A design of dried material, using a shell or sea material as
           container or accessory.

CLASS VI   *"And he made him (Joseph) a coat of many colors."* Genesis
           37:3

           A mass design of fresh flowers and foliage using several
           colors.

CLASS VII *"Let your light so shine. . . ."* Matthew 5:16

           A design using a candle, showing a strong contrast of
           black and white. Sprayed material permitted.

CLASS VIII *"They presented unto him (the wee one) gifts; gold. . . ."*
           Matthew 2:11

           A. Fresh plant material in a gold colored container.

B. All dried plant material, using a touch of gold. Gold
spray permitted.

CLASS IX　　*"Off To Church We Go."*

Informal corsages, ribbon permitted but plant material
must be dominant. Clipped foliage may be used.
A. All fresh plant material—4 Entries.
B. All dried plant material—4 Entries.

THE CHRISTMAS STORY (Using Christmas Carols and Scriptures)

I. O COME, ALL YE FAITHFUL　Isaiah 9:2—6:7—11:14
. . . For unto us a child is born . . . *Featuring worship.*

II. O LITTLE TOWN OF BETHLEHEM　St. Luke 1: 26-33—2:15
Joseph and Mary went into Bethlehem. *Featuring travel.*

III. THE ANGELS SONG　St. Luke 2:8-14
The angel said to the Shepherds, "Behold I bring you good
tidings of great joy . . . unto you a savior is born." *Featuring the
Shepherds.*

IV. IT CAME UPON THE MIDNIGHT CLEAR　St. Luke 2:15-20
And they came with haste and found Mary and Joseph, and the
babe lying in a manger. *Featuring Manger Scene.*

V. WE THREE KINGS OF ORIENT ARE　St. Matthew 2:7-12
. . . Herod sent the three wise men to Bethlehem to search for
the young child . . . *Featuring Wise Men.*

VI. HARK! THE HERALD ANGELS SING　St. Luke 2:10-14
. . . 'Glory to God in the highest, and on earth peace, good will
toward men. *Featuring peace—Symbol, dove.*

VII. SILENT NIGHT, HOLY NIGHT　St. Matthew 1:22-25
Written by Father Mohr, played on a guitar for Midnight Mass
by Franz Gruber in the Church of St. Nicholas in Oberndorf in
the Austrian Alps. (1787-1863.) *Featuring music accessories.
Could be guitar, violin, etc.*

Bibliography

ARNETT, DESSIE ASH and CLARK, LENANCE ROBINETTE. *Methodist Altars,* Nashville: Methodist Publishing House, 1961.

CIRLOT, J. E. *A Dictionary of Symbols,* New York: Philosophical Library, Inc., 1962.

CORSWANT, W. *A Dictionary of Life in Bible Times,* New York: Oxford University Press, 1960.

FERGUSON, GEORGE. *Signs and Symbols in Christian Art,* New York: Oxford University Press, 1959.

FREEHOF, LILLIAN S. and BANDMAN, LOTTIE C. *Flowers and Festivals of the Jewish Year,* New York: Hearthside Press, Inc., 1964.

LORTZIER, ROBERT P. and HUNTINGTON, HELEN. *Seasons and Symbols— A Handbook of the Church,* Minneapolis: Augsburg Publishing House, 1962.

STAFFORD, THOMAS ALFRED. *Christian Symbolism in the Evangelical Churches,* Nashville: Abingdon Press, 1942.

WALKER, WINIFRED. *All the Plants of the Bible,* New York: Harper and Row, 1957.

WILLIAMS, ALBERT N., (ed.). *Key Words of the Bible,* New York: Duell, Sloan & Pearce, Inc., 1956.

Index

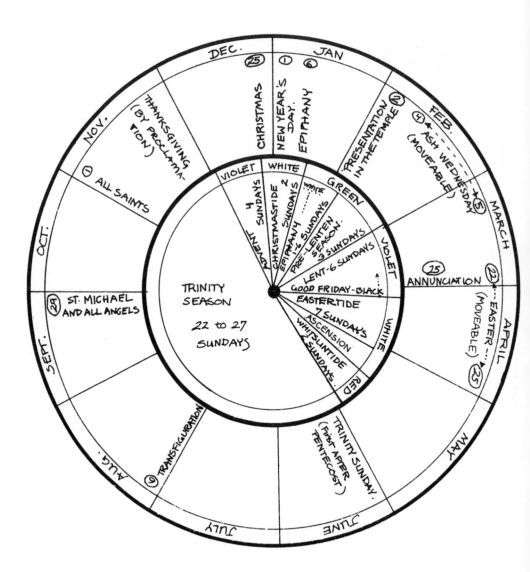